Hearts and Hands and Voices

*Music in the education of
slow learners*

DAVID WARD

LONDON
OXFORD UNIVERSITY PRESS
NEW YORK   TORONTO

circ,
Music

Oxford University Press, Walton Street, Oxford OX2 6DP

OXFORD   LONDON   GLASGOW   NEW YORK
TORONTO   MELBOURNE   WELLINGTON   CAPE TOWN
IBADAN   NAIROBI   DAR ES SALAAM   LUSAKA
KUALA LUMPUR   SINGAPORE   JAKARTA   HONG KONG   TOKYO
DELHI   BOMBAY   CALCUTTA   MADRAS   KARACHI

ISBN 0 19 314921 4

Printed in Great Britain
By the Camelot Press Ltd., Southampton

Preface

This handbook is the first-fruit of the national project, Music for Slow Learners: I hope all who are responsible for work with slow-learning children will find it of real value. The major report which is to follow it will be the culmination of eight years' teaching and investigation.

During these years we have lost two valued friends—Professor J. W. Tibble, Emeritus Professor of Education in the University of Leicester, who joined us in 1961 and from the first day identified himself with us at all levels of the project; his guidance, wisdom, and example were an inspiration to all who worked with him; and Raymond Roberts, Staff Inspector for Music at the D.E.S. for an all too short a period, another stalwart friend; without doubt his support for our work gained recognition and opportunities for it over a wide field.

To Jack Dobbs, the Director of the project, our debt is immense; from the earliest days whilst the project was still a dream, his concern for it was stimulating and played a major part in its establishment; his unceasing labour and relentless standards have played an equally large part in our achievement. To David Ward, the organizer of the project and a close colleague for eight years, we owe a great deal; his single-minded devotion, his deep understanding of our children, and his wise guidance have placed many in his debt, not least myself.

And finally, to my Committees I must express both thanks and gratitude for their constant encouragement and willing response to any demands upon them; their constant challenge has been a rare privilege for me.

Richard L. Bishop
Chairman of the Music for Slow Learners
Project Steering Committee

The following bodies gave generous financial help to the project:

> The Carnegie United Kingdom Trust
> The Clarkson Foundation
> The Leverhulme Trust Fund
> The John S. Cohen Foundation
> The Sidbury Trust
> The Eleanor Hamilton Educational Trust
> The Musicians' Union
> The Elmgrant Trust

and to them, and to our numerous private benefactors, we are deeply indebted.

The Standing Conference for Amateur Music and Oxford University Press acknowledge with gratitude a grant in aid from the Carnegie United Kingdom Trust towards the cost of production of this book.

The final report of the project is available from Dartington College of Arts, Totnes, South Devon, from whom full details can be obtained.

Contents

Illustrations

(between pp. 72 and 73)

Grateful thanks are due to the parents and teachers of the children whose photographs appear here for permission to use the illustrations, and most of all, of course, to the children themselves. Photographs by Neil Cooper.

Introduction

The material contained in this handbook for teachers is based
on the author's own teaching experience and on the experience
he has gained as organiser of the MUSIC FOR SLOW LEARNERS
project. This project, which was initiated by the Standing
Conference for Amateur Music and sponsored by the Carnegie
United Kingdom Trust, was established at Dartington College of
Arts, Devon, in 1968. It aimed to examine the special contribution music can make to the education of slow-learning children—
those found in special schools for educationally sub-normal and
physically handicapped pupils, in special classes of primary and
secondary schools, and in centres and hospitals for severely sub-
normal children. To this end, a number of research projects
were initiated, including experimental teaching and long-term
studies of the musical abilities of mentally handicapped,
educationally sub-normal, and cerebral palsied children, and a
survey of music activities in special schools in several parts of
the United Kingdom.

From the outset, teachers' courses were organised in order to
disseminate ideas and information arising out of the research as
early as possible. The most important of these courses, a one
term full-time course, received the approval and support of the
Department of Education and Science and became part of the
regular programme of teachers' courses at Dartington College
of Arts. The part-time tutors who worked on the annual termly
and shorter courses were remarkably generous in sharing their
own experience and ideas, and much of the material contained
in the following pages is derived from them.

I am indebted to all who allowed their school music activities
to be observed and recorded and to the project's Steering
Committee, some members of which were teaching colleagues
who gave constant encouragement and support. Most of all, I am
grateful to the many children who so cheerfully co-operated in
the experimental activities. The names used in this book are not,
of course, the real names of the children with whom I have
worked—and without whom this book could not have been written.

1 Background

The term *slow learners* will be frequently used in the pages
which follow. This term covers a very wide range of ability and
attainment—from the youngest severely sub-normal children to
the sixteen-year old pupils in secondary school special classes.
It includes a significant number of physically handicapped
children—particularly the cerebral palsied and those with spina
bifida—many of whom have both generalised and specific learning
difficulties. Slow learning children can be found in most schools,
but our concern here is with those who have been assessed and
who receive special educational treatment. Many of the music
activities which are suggested are based on practical experience
and observation of educationally sub-normal school children,
presently designated as 'mild' and who, in English schools, tend
to fall within the range of intelligence quotients from about 50
to 75. Special school teachers who read these suggestions will
realise that it is very difficult to relate any one group of slow
learning children to another, but it is hoped that the descriptions of the school situations will be sufficiently precise to assure
the readers of the possibilities of drawing information and ideas
from them in order to use and adapt in their own situations.

Slow-learning children tend to be noticed in their early years
of schooling because they show a marked backwardness in
reading, reading readiness, and language skills. Many of them
also demonstrate a marked degree of unwillingness or inability
to conform to the behaviour pattern which is expected of the
class group in which they are first placed. The reading, language,
and behaviour problems are usually inter-related.

Before they are placed in a special class or school, they are
normally given a series of tests to assess their level of development. The mental ability shown in these tests is usually compared
with the children's actual age and computed as an intelligence
quotient. In spite of educationists' many reservations about the
usefulness of IQ scores, these are treated very seriously by those
who are responsible for placing the children.

Most teachers are aware that intelligence tests only 'tap' a limited number of abilities. They also know that the children who are grouped according to any particular range of IQ scores have widely ranging abilities, especially where art, music, drama, physical education, and mechanical work are concerned. Also, there are great differences in the way these children behave in social situations.

There are many factors which contribute to slow learning. Special school teachers generally agree that a major cause is poverty of all kinds of stimulation in the very early years of life. Some learning problems can easily be traced to a definite sensory or organic disorder which may or may not be clearly connected with environmental factors.

Whatever the causes, there are certain approaches which are applicable to a large number of slow learning children, e.g. practical activities initiated on individual lines. The children's all-round needs must be considered, and most schools would aim to help their children to develop all their abilities as far as possible.

Music can make a unique contribution to meet the needs of these children. It can help them to realise their full potential. Through participation in a wide variety of music activities, they can be helped to become more aware of themselves and of others. Music can stimulate most of the senses, particularly the aural sense, it can facilitate communication, it can provide a sense of achievement which in turn brings an increase of self-confidence, and it can provide a means of enjoyable co-operation with others. By performing music to others, slow learning children can experience the joy of giving pleasure to others; for many of them, the opportunity to do so presents itself only rarely. With all these children it is necessary to make provision for musical activity in great breadth and variety. If music is seen only as a subject to be taught, or in terms of learning to play an instrument, then we shall be depriving the majority of our children of the enjoyment and educational benefits of musical participation. Nevertheless, a considerable number of slow learning children *can* learn a great deal about music and *can* learn to play instruments to a good standard, given the opportunity and appropriate teaching. Enormous satisfaction is gained from the playing of musical instruments and experience has shown that a general increase in self-confidence develops as a result of the particular sense of achievement which instrumental playing brings. This increased self-confidence is quite vital for children who have experienced failure in other aspects of their school work. Also, the playing of musical instruments helps physical and sensory co-ordination, develops the aural sense in particular, and stimulates intellectual activity. Most of all, it provides children with a possible means of future recreation and opens up avenues for enjoying a wider social life.

Realistically, we must recognise that the majority of our slow learning children will not become sufficiently skilled on instruments to enable them to play in school and youth orchestras. But music can be equally beneficial for those who do not reach sufficiently high standards to play in these rather specialized groups. Sound and rhythm reach the innermost depths of children, regardless of intellect and background; thus communication is possible where more obvious ways—e.g., spoken language—elicit little or no response. Many very simple musical activities using voices and instruments can give the children enjoyment both individually and in groups. The sense of achievement gained by more expert players is equally felt by those children whose condition makes it possible to play only a few chime bars or a simple drum rhythm. And through the many songs they can learn, the ear is developed, vocabulary enriched, rhythmic sense fostered, and knowledge about people, countries, and natural phenomena extended.

Teachers will, of course, be concerned with the *quality* of the activities they initiate. By encouraging the children to practise good techniques and to aim for a sincere and sensitive performance, a respect and love for music of all kinds will be imparted. But 'good' music activities may also be evaluated from the standpoint of the children's needs. In a schools' music survey conducted by the Music for Slow Learners project, all the answers given by the teachers to the question, 'what is the value of your music lessons with the children?' related specifically to these needs. They said: 'music is absolutely essential for emotional satisfaction'; 'it helps concentration and group disciplines'; 'it provides a stimulus for self-expression'; 'it gives the least able child an opportunity for success'; 'it helps motor co-ordination'; 'music time is a civilising, thoughtful time'. These are just a few of the many answers which seem to sum up the teachers' attitudes towards the use of music. If the actual activities in progress realise their aims, then a favourable evaluation can be made as a basis for future work. Interestingly, not many teachers felt that the long term future needs of the children should condition the curriculum; this may have been a deliberate omission. Clearly, the children should develop skills of performance and knowledge about music so that they will come to love the art, whether their present or future needs are to be met.

Whilst the concept of present *needs* is essential to help teachers plan and organise activities for the children, an overall scheme is often requested by teachers who rightly feel that their children should make 'progress'. The problem about designing such a scheme is the great number of directions in which progress is possible when music is used as an educational tool—as is suggested. It is, however, helpful—particularly in the early stages— to have a developmental framework which implies a knowledge of how young children grow through the various stages, both generally and musically. Unfortunately, little is known about early musical development but it is helpful to remind ourselves of certain facts.

The development of music in early childhood

Two musical components are present before the baby is born, and at the moment of birth—*sound* and *pulse*. It is fairly certain that the foetus is stimulated in various ways by the mother's heartbeat (pulse), and by her regular movements—e.g. walking and swimming. Nordoff and Robbins[1] make much use of the effect of different pulse rates in their work in music therapy with individual handicapped children. Other workers who deal with severely handicapped children use close bodily contact and rocking and swaying movements to try to stimulate a response in them. Rocking a baby seems to be a natural parental instinct; it is possible that babies who were not cuddled and rocked start out with musical deprivation.

It can be shown that the developing foetus at a certain stage can be stimulated to move when particular sounds are made near the mother's body.[2] Very shortly after birth, a baby will display the 'startle' reflex when sudden loud sounds are made nearby. It is fascinating to see this reflex action, which seems to explode from the very centre of the baby, spreading outwards through the limbs, hands, and fingers. In the early weeks of life normal babies respond interestingly to the sound of mother's voice—by becoming quite still or by turning the head towards the sound—and to the sound of approaching footsteps, running bathwater, feeding preparations, and bell sounds.[3] These early sounds and responses have an emotional meaning mostly associated with the baby's need for warmth, food, and security, and as such can be regarded as musical experiences.

The baby's first cry is fully charged with meaning! We can assume that this primeval action has great psychological importance as well as its physiological implications. Here, at this exciting moment is the principle of feedback—the baby is telling itself in no uncertain way, 'here I am'. Around the age of 24 weeks, the baby explores a variety of vocal sounds—'goo', 'bu-bu-bu', 'da-da', 'm-m-m' as a necessary preliminary stage to speech and singing.

From the age of about nine months a degree of control can be detected in the baby's beating movements which are made by using the whole arm on the side of the pram or cot. Also at this stage we can observe the beginnings of dancing—i.e. a rhythmic bouncing from the trunk and limbs to music which is sung or played nearby. Again, the parental instinct is to bounce the baby on the knee ('dandling' in the North Country) often accompanied by rhymes and songs, e.g. 'A farmer went trotting', 'Ladies go nim-nim-nim'.

The beginnings of melody seem to happen around the age of eighteen months. At this age, the baby will try to complete the endings of nursery rhymes—e.g. 'three bags full' and 'lives down the lane' (Baa baa black sheep), first vocalising the rhythm and then modulating the voice in approximation to the melody. Once this beginning has been made, there seems to be no end to the variety of short songs which can be learnt. All that is needed is a pattern to imitate. Some young children are deprived of the experience of hearing and repeating nursery rhymes; many slow-learning children in particular tend to miss this experience and it is necessary for the reception class teacher in the school to spend time bridging this gap.

Very little is known about the ability of pre-school children to begin to pick out tunes on a keyboard or glockenspiel. Certain children seem to be able to find melodies and even add 'correct' harmonies as early as three years; others seem particularly slow to demonstrate any musical ability. It is possible that precocious musical performance indicates a highly specialised ability which may emerge almost in spite of environmental influences; however, we do know that for many, musical expertise can be acquired through consistent teaching, opportunity, and persistence. As in many other areas of learning, parental interest and influence are very important factors. Some great teachers, e.g. Suzuki, believe that instrumental teaching should begin as early as possible, but clearly this can only apply in the case of certain instruments.

A number of studies have been carried out to discover whether or not musical ability correlates with general intelligence.[4] Most of these have been abortive in view of the complexities of assessing and reliably testing both these areas. Casual observations show that certain children of low mental ability can perform surprisingly well in particular kinds of musical activity— e.g. playing 'by ear'. This appears to support the view that certain musical abilities are very specific and one is tempted to suspect that these are innate. In practice, it is important for the teacher to recognise how the children function in the classroom situation and to organise the music activity in such a way that each child is making a contribution appropriate to his needs and abilities. It is, of course, equally important to recognise particular individual talents and to try to make additional provision for suitable musical tuition.

The teacher

What sort of qualities and skills are needed by those who teach music to slow-learning children?

It has already been suggested that the teacher should have a good working knowledge of the possible causes of the learning difficulties of the children she teaches and a sensitivity to their overall needs. She should also know about child development, especially in the earliest stages and be able to see how the individuals in her class relate to the known patterns of development. Where the teaching of music is concerned, it is especially important for her to know about these early stages of development. However, her musical responsibility in special education will extend far beyond the level of nursery and infant activities, so she will need to have a good personal standard of musical skill, a wide background knowledge, and much teaching expertise. But there is no direct relationship between the degree of the teacher's own *instrumental* skill and her ability to initiate activities with the children. Some musicians with extensive qualifications and skills find it difficult to adapt their own expertise to the needs and abilities of slow learners. Others with very little personal executive skill are able, by careful organisation, preparation, and enthusiasm to produce extremely good results with the children. Patience, optimism, consistency of approach, and good control and organisation are needed as well as a varied repertoire of songs and simple instrumental pieces, the ability to teach songs quickly and effectively, a basic knowledge of chords and the devising of accompaniments, and a working experience of school percussion and other simple instruments. Most of all, the teacher must enjoy music and be sensitive to an infinite variety of musical idioms and ways in which music can be experienced and performed.

It is essential that children's musical efforts should be heard and appreciated by others and that the teacher should be given warm recognition for her work. Here, the school's head-teacher has a vital role to play in displaying a sincere interest in and recognition of the value of musical activity for the children. So much good work goes unnoticed in schools, and nothing is more counter-productive than an indifferent or sceptical head-teacher. The head's role, in practical terms, is also to make it possible for groups to be formed and taught at suitable times and in suitable places and to help to provide good instruments and equipment.

Whenever possible, the teacher should engage in musical and other activities outside school and at her own adult level. The teaching of music is very demanding of physical and emotional energy, and she will need periodic refreshment which can be gained from outside activities. She should be encouraged to attend courses frequently and these courses need to have a strong element of activity which is designed to contribute to her own personal development. It is vital that the the teacher should continue to grow and develop in her own area of activity. In this way she will remain aware of the children's needs to develop and come to her class with enthusiasm and vigour.

Notes

[1] P. Nordoff and C. Robbins *Therapy in music for handicapped children* Gollancz
[2] Rosamund Shuter *The psychology of music* Methuen
[3] Mary Sheridan *The developmental progress of infants and young children* HMSO pamphlet no. 102
[4] Rosamund Shuter *The psychology of music* (Appendix III) Methuen

2 Music activities with young slow-learning children

The first priorities with the youngest children will be to get them singing and moving. It is likely that most of them will have little or no experience of nursery rhymes and simple action songs. Also, they may not be ready for group teaching. Much work on individual lines is necessary and here it may be possible to enlist the help of the classroom aide. To encourage group activity, it is helpful to adopt the nursery school technique of having a definite time, or section of the room for songs and stories. Some children will soon come to enjoy this routine and acquire the habit of being ready to take part in the songs. Young children respond well to the teacher's own singing voice which should not be artificially produced, but a natural part of her own personality. If the teacher is just not confident enough to use her singing voice it is possible for her to use records or tapes. This, however, is only second best. Her own voice will re-inforce the relationship which should be developing with the children.

Songs should be pitched within a comfortable range—e.g. from about middle C to D′ (fourth line of the treble clef), although it should be remembered that songs have their own particular 'lie', and higher notes are sometimes sung more easily if approached in certain musical ways. Generally speaking, most song books present songs in keys which are too high for our children; the teacher should therefore be wary of using these books except to learn the songs for herself. For the youngest children, accompaniments are often quite unsuitable, and even at best can be distracting. If she is an accomplished guitarist, then by all means she should use her instrument for accompaniment, but again she should be wary of making the song fit the particular chords which come easily on the instrument.

The Oxford nursery song book (Oxford University Press) contains an excellent collection of English nursery rhymes. *American folk songs for children* (Doubleday) also contains very good songs, many of which have appropriate actions for this age group. Songs like 'Johny get your hair cut' are suitable for making up verses to fit the mood of the moment or to make an

individual appeal to the children. This song also lends itself to
mime. Each verse—e.g. 'Johnny put your tie on'—can be mimed
by the teacher and the children either before or during the verse.
Every opportunity should be taken to encourage the children to
move in their music activities. Indeed, it is hardly possible to
have music without some sort of movement. They need plenty
of opportunities to clap the pulse of songs and the rhythm of
certain words and phrases which occur in the songs. When they
are familiar with several nursery rhymes they can be asked to
guess the name of the rhyme from the rhythm alone. There is a
stage with some children when they can speak a rhythm but are
still unable to clap it. For these, the teacher might experiment
with vocal sounds based on the rhythm of the songs they know.
Walking the pulse of a song is also a useful activity. This is
perhaps best done in a secure circular formation and could easily
develop into a simple country dance. Thus, 'Twinkle, twinkle
little star' could become a simple dance in which the children
take four steps anti-clockwise to the first line of the tune, four
steps clockwise to the second line, make four high claps to the
third and fourth lines, and a reverse turn on the spot for the last
two lines. Traditional singing games such as 'Oats and beans and
barley grow' and 'Poor Mary lies a-weeping' are much enjoyed
by all young children; the teacher may have to present these
games, which are normally learnt from older children in the
playground. She might enlist the help of colleagues to refresh
her own memory of the singing games she enjoyed in early child-
hood, or refer to the excellent collection made by Peter and Iona
Opie—*Children's games in street and playground* (Oxford
University Press). Additional books and records are listed in
Appendix II.

The introduction of instruments

Instruments should be introduced very gradually. It is better for
these children to have just one good quality xylophone or
glockenspiel at first, rather than a complete range of percussion.
The teacher is advised to practise using the instrument herself,
and should be able to play tunes which are familiar to the children

and make interesting sound effects. The youngest children seem to need occasions when they can fix their attention on just one small thing; they can be easily over-stimulated by having too many instruments. One of the best lessons the author observed was centred entirely on a tuning fork. The children thought it was almost magical because it could sing 'silently' to its master, or sing aloud through a table or even tickle the end of their noses when the vibrating prongs were placed very lightly on them. These children are often very curious—sometimes about things we don't particularly want them to be—and if a sense of expectation is built up, they can become quite involved with the object or sound we wish to present. Good use can be made of this curiosity when introducing them to new things, or when they are encouraged to be excited about beautiful sounds and natural phenomena. These may be very close at hand; slow-learning children are frequently quite unaware of the bird songs, flowers, and trees which are within a few yards of their class-room window.

Try listening at very close range to a cymbal struck quietly with a soft beater. If it is a good quality instrument, the low, booming frequencies will be heard. Let the children hear these unusual sounds by holding the instrument over their heads, or quite close to their ears. Perceptive teachers will perhaps wish to use intensive listening lessons diagnostically; it is sometimes possible to discover hearing or perceptual problems in the music sessions where clinical examinations have failed to reveal specific problems.

Use the percussion instruments to make evocative sounds to enrich a story. Avoid overdoing this, but certain well chosen sounds can make a story or poem come alive. *The three billy goats Gruff* (Ladybird books) is a story which lends itself to the addition of sounds. Choose three different sounds for the big, middle-sized, and little goats—e.g. a tambour, a stringed dulcimer and a small triangle. The troll can be represented by a cymbal; this, with the tambour, will represent a very exciting fight scene at the end of the story! Invent a rhythmic phrase for the troll to repeat—e.g. 'who's walking over my bridge?'

—and get the children to chant this each time the goats cross the bridge. Animal sounds and movements are easily represented by percussive sounds. Any small, hopping creature can be 'played' by using hard beaters on the xylophone (make them 'hop'); snakes and fishes can be illustrated by smooth glissandi on the same instrument. A wood-block makes an excellent ticking clock, and wire brushes on a snare drum can produce a realistic steam train sound. The stories do not necessarily have to be traditional. A simple series of events which happen to a boy or girl with whom the children will easily identify can be very meaningful to them. Sounds for coming downstairs can be played on the xylophone or glockenspiel, traffic sounds can be made with a variety of instruments, and walking or running music can be invented on the drums. Do not expect that all the children in the group will immediately understand the point of this work. It is wise at first for the teacher to make the sounds and then choose particular children to make certain sounds. They may need to be shown how to do this. If we wait for the children to be spontaneous or 'original', some of them will never take part.

Much use can be made of sounds without relating them to stories, animals, or events. Modern school percussion instruments make beautiful and interesting sounds in themselves, and these, thoughtfully presented, will open the children's ears, make them more alert, and encourage them to be discriminating and selective. Games can be played in which the children identify the instrument which is played behind a screen; everyday objects may also be used in this game. In 1800, Dr. Itard[1] used this technique to reach Victor, the 'wild' boy of Aveyron, through the aural sense. It is interesting to note that this boy responded especially keenly to survival sounds—e.g. a breaking twig, or a nut being cracked.

With very handicapped children, activities might well be based on the sound/response idea for much of the time. Remember that the earliest developmental responses are quite simple movements relating to meaningful sounds. Try using a variety of single sounds at varying distances and with varying degrees of loudness. The children are required to point to the sound source, or to turn and look at it. For more able children, the game can be developed to a high level of complexity by making several sounds simultaneousl

and asking them to identify them. Then, a sequence of sounds—
at first just two or three—can be played, and the children asked
to say, or indicate by pointing, which came first, second, and
so on. The teacher may be very surprised at the varying abilities
of the children to make the correct response in this activity.
It will be seen that this ability is analogous to the phonic
blending we ask them to do later on in their reading lessons.
This activity also has diagnostic possibilities for speech and
language activities; it is possible that some of the children's
problems may be caused by a variety of difficulties connected
with weak perception at the input or organizational stage, and
until this is remedied to some extent we cannot expect correct
responses at the output stage. Rhythm is probably also connected
with this aspect of functioning. We know that certain children
who stutter or stammer can be helped to become more fluent
by song and poetry. It seems that the security of the rhythm
helps to overcome the neurological or emotional difficulties of
the halting speaker. Teachers might like to experiment with the
sequencing of sounds presented in a clear rhythmic pattern, as
well as presenting them a-rhythmically. An intermediate stage
in this work could involve the vocal imitation of the sounds
which are presented. The children might be able to say, for
example, 'boom, ting, tick' instead of 'drum, bell, wood-block'.

Many games which involve the use of sound can be invented.
Consider the many sound qualities at our disposal, the varying
degrees of loudness and ways of playing them, and the directions
and distances involved between the ear and the sound source.
It is possible to devise a whole programme of work on this aspect
of music-making. The children might move towards the sound,
'grow' with a crescendo of sound, curl up to a downward scale
or diminuendo, or move smoothly for 'smooth' (legato) sounds
and jerkily to staccato sounds. Simple party games—e.g. 'hunt
the slipper', 'how green you are', 'musical chairs', 'squeak piggy',
'steal the keys', and 'pass the parcel' (using an instrument)—can
all be adapted to involve the use of simple sounds.

The teacher should realise that, although her slow-learning
children may function very well in these simple activities with
sound, they need a long enough period of time to assimilate the

learning of many of the musical concepts which are incidentally presented to them. All the instruments, whether tuned or untuned, make sounds which are recognizably high or low when compared with, or related to, each other. A triangle makes a higher sound, or more correctly a cluster of higher sounds, than a tambour. Maracas and classroom-made shakers make sounds which differ in pitch—compare the sound of a rice-filled plastic container with one which has dried peas in it—and, by focusing the children's attention on these different instruments and the sounds they make, we are reinforcing their concepts of pitch. Children are sometimes written off as unmusical because they sing on a monotone. These same children are frequently able to discriminate so finely as to recognise the difference between salt and sugar-filled containers.

The teacher may wish to encourage the children to add simple instrumental sounds to their songs. Often, the younger children are not sufficiently mature to cope with singing and playing at once. If they do so, keep the instrumental parts very simple. Songs like 'The gay musician'[2] and 'Let everyone clap hands like me' or 'We'll all clap hands together' have a natural rhythmic break which allows for definite sounds to be included where the break occurs. Some teachers, in their natural anxiety to get the children fully involved, try to add too much too quickly to the songs—which may be of great interest in their own right—with the result that the effect is noisy and chaotic. Often, just one percussion instrument is sufficient to provide rhythmic or tonal interest.

The foundations of instrumental work will be laid in this work with the youngest children. They need to learn what sort of sounds the instruments can make, how to identify them, and how they can take on a variety of meanings. At some stage, the children need to explore the instruments for themselves, but the teacher may have much ground-work to do—showing them *how* to play, what to do, and most of all trying to transmit her own enthusiasm and care for the production of beautiful and interesting sounds in music. Children with considerable mental handicaps sometimes remember surprisingly well some of the exciting moments in their music sessions. The tuning fork lesson mentioned earlier was clearly remembered four years later by the children who were involved.

Listening to music

Every opportunity should be taken to play music, live and recorded, to the children. It is not a good idea to have randomly chosen music playing as a background to other activities. Muzak may have its purpose in the motorway café and on the railway station, but there is no evidence to show that this does any more than temper the mood of the moment. There should always be a definite reason for playing music, and it must be thoughtfully chosen and presented. Most of the young slow-learning children in our care have never experienced music other than the popular variety they hear on television, much of which is of secondary importance to the personalities and show business it relies on. Young children respond to colourful music and seem to need short, complete pieces whose shape they can 'feel'. Whenever possible, live music should be performed for them; this will probably have to be done by visiting peripatetic teachers, local bandsmen, or music students. Most large secondary schools in England now have school orchestras from which several good players can be drawn. Visiting instrumentalists and singers never cease to be impressed by the way ESN children respond to a good performance. The ability to recognise a technically correct and sincere interpretation seems to lie in all of us, irrespective of general intelligence and experience. All except the most professional of these visiting musicians will need to be advised on the length and nature of their pieces; if the children are allowed to touch the instrument, and even play a sound, all the better. The teacher needs to keep her ear to the ground for distinctive music to play on records or tape. For useful lists and examples of music see *Music, movement, and mime for children* by Vera Gray and Rachel Percival (Oxford University Press), and also *Dance and drama in education* by Vi Bruce (Pergamon). It cannot be too strongly stressed that the teacher must listen to the music first before deciding how and when to use it!

Pre-school experience

It is worth mentioning that some local education authorities in England have appointed advisory teachers who travel to the homes of handicapped children to work with them and their parents in preparation for admission to school. In one county area, at the time of writing, the teacher happens to be experienced in teaching music to ESN children and makes good use of song and simple instruments in their homes. In this way, the children have some experience and expectation of what might be offered when they go to school, and more important, the parents are involved and see the interesting way their children sometimes respond to music. This particular advisory service is closely linked with the local handicapped children's toy library, which contains some sturdy instruments and cassette tape recorders. Parents take their children along to the library, and in consultation with the teacher encourage them to try various toys and instruments which may then be borrowed for as long as the need exists. Sometimes a particular instrument appeals to a child, stimulating him in a very special way. For certain children with problems of communication and relationships, the tape recorder has produced surprising results.

Musical activity can sometimes provide the starting point for a new surge in development with young and severely handicapped children. We have reports of children who have spoken for the first time in the music session, perhaps because of their fascination with the instruments or equipment. One teacher discovered that she could give a difficult child instructions—which were obeyed!— through the tape recorder; others have found that some children will respond to questions when they are sung rather than spoken. Several cases are reported of children who never speak but who happily sing the verses of nursery rhymes quite clearly, and one teacher recently reported that her 'special care children' became quite animated at the sound of bagpipes!

At present we have little understanding of the processes which occur when responses are made to musical phenomena. What we do know is that music can sometimes produce responses which no other language can. This is at least a starting point for work with our children who are so much in need of stimulation.

Notes

1   Jacques Itard *The wild boy of Aveyron* Appleton Century Crofts
2   see Appendix II

3   Music with nine- to twelve-year-old slow-learning children

Most of the day-to-day problems encountered in many of our special schools are those associated with undesirable behaviour. Slow learning children grow and develop very erratically and at any given point in time the teacher can observe a wide range of developmental levels in any one child. Generally speaking, the greatest problems are caused where a child's emotional stage is out of step with his physical and mental levels. Tantrums in a heavy twelve year old are less easy to accept and deal with than in an infant.

Singing

Because music is a language of emotions, we can reason that it should be a useful activity to include in any school programme which aims to help emotional development. Certainly in our choice of songs and other musical material we can provide the children with a sense of growing up; by the age of ten they should be leaving nursery rhymes behind and we should be choosing songs for them with words which have universal appeal. Luckily, in music we do not have quite the same problem as in reading, where a very basic vocabulary must be retained. Through songs we can extend and enrich the vocabulary of our children and give them an immediate sense of the meaning of the words. Learning the words of songs comes surprisingly easily to them if the teaching is efficient and business-like.

A good many American and West Indian folk songs are suitable for this age group. 'When I first came to this land', 'The mocking bird', 'Mary had a baby', and 'Water come to me eye' are songs with easily understood language and can be performed in a present-day style. These children like songs which have a firm underlying beat and a comfortable vocal range. As with the younger children, we shall need to transpose songs down to avoid notes above D'. Teaching the songs phrase by phrase in rote patterning will make for speedy and efficient learning, but it will be very helpful for the children to have the words clearly displayed on large cards so that the children's heads are kept up. It goes without saying that the teacher should know the song thoroughly before giving it to the children. It is desirable to teach songs by vocal patterning; melodic support from the piano or other instruments should be kept to a minimum if the children are to gain vocal independence. Sometimes it is a good idea to begin teaching a song with the chorus, so that the children have a feeling of immediate success. Through repetition they will gradually learn the verses, but the teacher should make sure that the later verses are sufficiently rehearsed. Often so much work goes into the early verses of a song that the children are too tired or bored to learn the rest.

The piano is an excellent aid as long as the teacher is expert enough on the keyboard to enable her to look away from it whilst playing. Similarly, if a music copy is being used, it should not command all the teacher's attention. As a rule, accompaniments need to be simplified rather than expanded or decorated; their function is to state an introduction and then to lend harmonic and rhythmic support to the song, rather than to distract the attention from it. Some songs are much better accompanied by the guitar, autoharp, or the children's percussion instruments, and the possibility of unaccompanied singing should not be overlooked; many folk songs were, in their original state, unaccompanied. It is right to involve the children in playing their own accompaniments on the tuned percussion instruments, but this needs planning with care if sameness is to be avoided. Too many school songs with 'Orff' accompaniments can become remarkably boring!

The teacher, and the children, must be very sensitive about the addition of percussion instruments to a song accompaniment. Again, the effect should be to add interest and support rather than to distract. A light and clear effect is desirable. Many groups make the mistake of allowing the drummer to play every beat and giving the triangles too much to do. This results in a clumsy and irritating accompaniment. An exciting rhythm is achieved by leaving *out* the strong beats which should be easily felt by the performers in any case. If tambours are used, the possibility of tuning them should not be overlooked. A tambour tuned to the dominant note of the melody (i.e. soh) and played correctly will give an excellent timpani effect. Maracas are most effectively played crisply on the 'off' beat; the children may need to be shown how to play them by giving them a sharp tap with the forefinger to get this crisp effect. Cymbals are best used in song accompaniments to punctuate rather than to play the pulse, but they may also be played in a jazz style with wire brushes, and suspended from a stand; for this the player needs plenty of practice to produce a really clear beat. Phrases for xylophones and glockenspiels should be carefully arranged for ease of playing and so that they have the effect of bridging the phrases of the song. The children should be encouraged, where possible, to play with two matched beaters, and help may be needed from the teacher in the working out of alternate left- and right-hand patterns for any particular phrase. If possible, all the bars should be left on the xylophones and glockenspiels unless the children are quite unable to remember which ones to play or to co-ordinate their hands and beaters on the correct bars. By leaving all the bars on we are helping to build up a concept of the scales in common use; this is a valuable part of their musical education.

A list of well-tried songs is included in Appendix II. It is hoped that the music teacher will collect her own repertoire of songs which can be culled from almost any source. Slow-learning children are usually remarkably open-minded about the songs they like to sing. These can be currently popular, from musical shows, of folk or spiritual origin, or from the classical repertoire. Generally speaking, songs which the teacher really likes and is convinced about are taught most effectively. An optimistic and enthusiastic teacher can put over almost anything she wishes.

What sort of vocal tone should we expect from the children? Although some individuals have beautiful voices, group singing is frequently rather coarse. We must not expect anything like a cathedral choirboy sound; on the other hand, we do not accept shouting. Perhaps the best solution is to exploit the lower range of their voices (sometimes known as the chest voice)—in any case we shall be pitching their songs in low keys. Luckily, much of their singing material is likely to be vigorous and therefore a lusty sound is right. 'What shall we do with the drunken sailor?'

would sound odd if sung with a choirboy tone. A mellow
accompaniment helps to set the scene for quieter and sweeter
singing, and clearly, less vigorous songs will elicit appropriate
treatment if care is taken to help the children understand the
meaning of the words.

Monotone singers, or growlers, rightly worry many teachers,
and existing literature gives many neat recipes to overcome the
problem. The trouble is that the recipes do not necessarily work
with our children. The monotone may be caused by a variety of
problems—faulty perception, poor reproducing mechanisms, or
just plain carelessness. It is certain that withdrawing them from
the singing group will not help them, and the net result of this
will-be that the group will become progressively smaller! Some
teachers make sure that the poor singers are placed next to good
singers; others take the growlers aside and try to find their 'own'
note, match it with the piano or the teacher's voice and try to
get them to move upwards. It may be easier for some children
to move downwards first. Certainly we need to encourage them
to feel the physical sensation of a moving voice; then we can
begin to aim for some control. One excellent teacher was
observed with her choir grouped in small circles, facing inwards
so that the facial expressions as well as the voices of the good
singers helped the weaker ones. After all, it is probably only
convention and the need for the teacher to see the singers which
makes us set them out all facing the front.

Ideally, the children need to have singing sessions several
times each week. The teacher will know from experience how
long these sessions should last, and it might be possible to balance
the time spent on singing with other music activities such as are
suggested later.

It is hardly necessary to emphasize the value of singing for
all our children. J. P. B. Dobbs writes fully about the physical
and other benefits of singing in his book *The slow learner and
music* (Oxford University Press), and those who are interested
in historical writings on music education will often find singing
included under the heading *Physical education*! But anyone who
has sung with choirs and groups knows the exhilarating feeling
which comes with singing. We sing when we feel happy and vice

versa. The greater part of the lives of many of our slow-learning children is spent in drabness. Even if momentary enjoyment were the only benefit, then the singing sessions would be valuable.

Instrumental work

If there is progression in the school's music programme, then by the time the children reach the age of nine or ten they should be ready for group instrumental work. If the children at this stage have had no instrumental experience, it will probably be necessary to take them back through some of the activities suggested in the previous chapter. Just as with the younger children, it can be disastrous suddenly to introduce a whole range of exciting instruments to them.

With this middle school group it is wise to present the instruments gradually, exercising a very firm control of the children right from the start. They will probably need to be shown how to handle and care for the instruments. This is not only economically sensible, but also a way of instilling a sense of care for good things—which many of them need to learn. At first, there should be occasions when the children are invited to come out individually and show the rest how well they can handle the instruments and make interesting sounds on them. Begin with the bass xylophone, or with the biggest xylophone available. This is an impressive instrument and it should elicit a sense of privilege, which in turn implies care. They may need to be shown how to strike the bars correctly, how to make ascending and descending glissandi and to play very simple tunes. Most children like to pick out 'Baa, baa black sheep', 'Jingle bells' and the first few notes of the national anthem.

When most of the instruments have been introduced the children can enjoy some of the sound games already mentioned, and the teacher can expect a more alert and controlled response in these games. The games which follow are excellent for encouraging finer discrimination and control, and should prepare the children for later work which is of a more creative nature.

Who played?

Seat the children in a circle, each with an instrument. Select a child to come out, cover his eyes, and give a signal for one of the players to produce a quiet sound. The aim is for the 'guesser' to point to that player. The game may be developed by having more than one player make a sound (at the same time), and also by asking the guesser to name the player and his instrument. Here, the correct names of the instruments should be used. They will enjoy using new words such as 'glockenspiel' and 'guiro'.

Conversations

This is a well-tried activity in which the children are again seated in circular formation, each with an instrument. The object of the game is to pass musical sounds around and across the circle. One child begins by making any sounds she wishes, then invites another, by nodding, to produce her 'statement' in sound. The second child makes her sounds then invites another to play and so on. No speaking is allowed—this encourages eye contact amongst the children, and ensures that each contribution is heard by everyone. The children teach each other by imitation and by discovering new ways of creating their sounds, and they become familiar with the qualities of sounds the instruments make. The social aspect of this game is interesting. Certain children who are especially popular tend to get more turns to play, but after a few sessions a 'musical popularity' emerges with some groups. Particular children discover that they can play very inventively and the group tends to respect this inventiveness by giving more turns to these players. The complexity of this game may be increased by having two separate musical statements to begin a round of conversation. This makes all the participants extremely alert and watchful; they do not like to miss their turn to play.

Adoption

Select four players and provide them each with a different

instrument. Make sure that the instruments are very strongly contrasted—e.g. cymbal, wood-block, tom-tom drum, and maraca. Either divide the rest of the class into four groups, or ask them to 'adopt', or choose, the instrument they wish to respond to. Then make sure that the players are hidden from the rest. The aim is for the children who are not players to move, in whichever way the teacher decides, only when 'their' adopted instrument plays. Encourage the instrumentalists to be economical in their playing, sometimes making sounds just one at a time and at other times with two, three, or four instruments sounding together. This game encourages awareness, alertness, and selectivity in all the participants. In a room which has plenty of space, the children who respond to the sounds will enjoy exploring large movements which express the kinds of sounds they are hearing. The cymbal might stimulate sustained, slow movements, the maraca will probably suggest quick, shaking movements, and the wood-block may encourage stiff and jerky movements. Further suggestions for moving in a large space will be given later in this chapter.

The two games, 'Who played?' and 'Adoption', can easily be adapted to teach pitch perception. Instead of the instruments suggested above, any number of chime bars may be used. It is wise, however, to begin with just two bars—the highest and the lowest in pitch—and have these positioned well apart in the room. At first the children can be asked to say who played, but later on they should be able to give the name of the sound, e.g. C or G. This can be made increasingly demanding by extending the range of bars and by decreasing the distance between them. If this is carefully graded in presentation the children will become surprisingly adept at naming the notes.

The thoughtful teacher will be able to organize many variations on these games and perhaps invent new ones. Remember that a definite aim should be borne in mind; the games are enjoyable in themselves, but we should all the time be looking for a development of the children's awareness, alertness, concentration, and discrimination.

Sensitivity is an additional aim and this can be encouraged to develop through further activities in which the instruments

are used to make a variety of sounds. It may be helpful in these
activities for the teacher to ignore the rhythm and pitch aspects
of music-making. Too many aims tend to make for a muddled
approach and a confusion in the minds of the children about
what is really expected of them. Through the simple games
there should develop a working facility with the instruments;
given this facility the children are ready to proceed to activities
which are, for them, original and creative.

Slow-learning children seem to need a very firm structure
within which they can make their original contributions. It is
very doubtful whether they will produce satisfying results if
they are simply given the instruments and told to 'make some
music', although the teacher should always be on the lookout
for individuals who do have constructive ideas on which group
activities may be based. When this happens, the teacher should
step in and suggest how these individual ideas might be used
and developed with the whole group. Some of the best activities
may happen in this way, but the teacher should not depend on
it entirely.

Composing with sound qualities

Divide the players into four groups, i.e. those whose instruments
make metallic sounds, drum sounds, wood sounds, and shaker
sounds. Using clear directions which involve hand signals to
show the players when to *start* and *stop*, invite each group to
play sounds whilst the rest listen. Ask the children about the
quality of the sounds they make, or what sort of things they
think of when the sounds are made, or help them by making
suggestions. Aim for quiet sustaining sounds from the metallic
instruments. These might suggest something which is airborne
or floating. The drums will probably suggest a more earthbound
and possibly aggressive feeling. The children should sense that
the four groups of sound have individual qualities and feelings
about them. Having demonstrated this point it is an easy step to
make a very simple composition—which should have a clear
beginning and end. The teacher's knowledge of simple musical
forms should help here; a simple binary or fourfold sequence,

or a rondo (A B A C A D A), might be attempted.

The groups of instruments or individual instruments can evoke associations with natural phenomena. Space travel is often associated with a strange mixture of metallic sounds—particularly those made by the cymbal and triangle when struck by soft beaters—and a story might be simulated in sounds. For the space journey the players will need to practise a very long crescendo which will tax their abilities to ensure a fine control over their instruments. Other topics and situations which lend themselves well to interpretation in sounds are: the sea, traffic, crowd scenes, ghosts and witches, a burglary, Cowboys and Indians, factories.

The imaginative aspect of sound making leads naturally into dramatic situations. The children enjoy drama which appeals to their primitive instincts, and the universal themes of hunting, war, and love are frequently chosen by them. Simple war dances will involve rhythmic drumming and chants which can easily be invented. Masks and totems can be made, and used to heighten the sense of the drama. Music used in this way relates to the fundamental needs and drives in all of us.

When the teacher is sufficiently confident in her ability to control the instrumental group, and when the children are able to use the instruments sensitively, improvisation with sounds is possible. Only those who have experienced musical improvisation know the tremendous sense of satisfaction which comes with this activity. Improvisation can be enjoyed in a variety of ways but in most of them a definite structure seems necessary. If we are given no guidelines whatever, it becomes very difficult even to make a start.

Arrange the children in a horseshoe formation, each with an instrument. Ensure that the instruments are capable of producing a wide variety of sounds—it is not easy to be expressive with a castanet! The teacher should be positioned well for conducting. By means of starting and stopping signals with the hands, invite individuals to play. Next, by means of various hand signals, try to get individual players to vary their contributions in terms of length, loudness or softness, smoothness, and pitch. Make sure that there are plenty of silent moments; silence is an important ingredient in music-making. Explore the interaction of different instruments and groups of instruments, and try to achieve a sense of climax and a clear ending. In this activity, the teacher will really be the improvisor. It might be helpful to devise a simple plan beforehand, e.g.

1   cymbals, triangles, and chime bars—play soft, sustained sounds
2   drums and tambours—soft, quickly repeated sounds
3   glocks and xylophones—many widely spread notes played quickly and shortly
4   all the instruments—a long, gradual crescendo
5   silence—for five seconds
6   cymbals, triangles, and chime bars—a long, gradual diminuendo

Selected children may conduct the group. Some of them will need an idea on which to base their improvisations; the sea and space travel topics are again useful and it might be possible to allow them to improvise with a very simple story or series of natural events in mind, e.g.

1   a man is walking down the street—drums play a walking pulse
2   he runs and throws a brick through a window—cymbal and triangles make a crashing sound
3   he gathers up silver and jewellery—glocks and chime bars make many short 'busy' sounds
4   he runs away, the police chase him, a crowd gathers—drums make running sounds, tambours join in, all instruments make quick busy noises

These improvisations with sounds may later be visually represented. The burglary might be quickly drawn both as (A) events in the story and (B) as musical patterns:

A

1   2   3   4

B

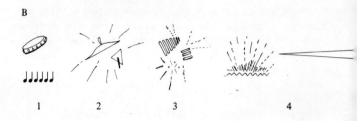

1   2   3   4

The sounds of words

In one ESN school, a class of ten-year-old children were
exploring onomatopoeic sounds. They had chosen the theme
water and were trying to think of as many words as possible
which suggested the sounds which water makes, e.g. drip, splash,
dribble, drop, trickle, pitter-patter. The actual sounds of water
were also listened to, and later a composition in simulated sound,
using instrumental and vocal effects, was made. Songs which
involve water were sung and simple phrases using the adjectives
associated with water were invented.

Water is an excellent theme as a basis for sound-making.
Glockenspiels can 'become' rivers, rice rolled around in a tambour
can realistically simulate the waves of the sea. Rain can be made
to tap on a roof by using a small drum or it can tipple down
with rice or corn pouring into a waste bin! It is fairly obvious to
children how they need to play for thunder and lightning. Real
water can be used to make rhythmic sounds by slapping its
surface. It can be used to change the pitch of a struck glass or
bottle by adding more or taking some away, and it can make a
vibrating gong or cymbal sound very mysterious if it is slowly
immersed whilst vibrating. The musical possibilities are considerably increased when the actions of rowing, winding, scrubbing,
and swimming are made to sea songs and shanties.

It will be seen that there is so much work possible using
sound games, compositions, and improvisations that an entire
music-making programme could be devised to run over a three
year period. The extent to which this is done will depend on the
teacher's own enthusiasm and the interest and capabilities of the

children. It is suggested that work with sounds is planned to take place alongside the other music activities and only the teacher can decide whether whole sessions are devoted to this or whether it is presented as just one part of a full music session, with singing and other activities to make a good balance. Ideally, over the school years, there should be gradual growth of all aspects of music activity; long-term growth and development is desirable.

Orff-Schulwerk

It would be wrong at this stage not to mention the work of Carl Orff and his followers in music education. Many of their techniques are very relevant to the needs and abilities of slow-learning children. In recent years they have been increasingly interested in the use of sound as a starting point in music education, but the majority of music teachers associate the name of Orff with the use of word rhythms and the pentatonic scale.

The musical connection with words is fairly obvious. A moment's reflection will remind us that every time we speak words and phrases we use the musical element, *rhythm*. The rhythm of words can be expressed in musical notation (at the risk of making them sound too mechanical). Thus, 'Tom, Tom the piper's son' may be written

We can speak the words in a precise rhythm or we might tap this rhythm on a table, or clap it, or play it on a percussion instrument. Alternatively, we might recreate it vocally by using different sounds from the original, e.g.

pom pom pi pom pom pom

With this kind of rhythmic work many individual and group activities are possible. Varied use of these rhythmic ideas is possible by performing them in sequence or by performing the original words together with the drum rhythm, or the tapping

with the clapping. Children quite naturally invent short rhythmic
chants in the playground or when they are walking to school.
This rhythm occurs very often:

and at the time of writing this chant is popular for some odd
reason:

$$\frac{2}{4} \; | \; ♩ \; ♫ \; | \; ♩ \; ♫ \; | \; ♩ \; ♩ \; | \; ♩ \;$$

run, rabbit, run, rabbit, run, run, run

James Blades, the well-known percussionist and teacher,
recommends the use of word rhythms to help players over
certain complex rhythmic patterns which are not immediately
clear when seen in musical notation, and the classical Indian
tabla (drum) players have their own system of word rhythms on
which they base many of their intricate patterns. We can assume
that any child who can speak words of more than one syllable
can express a rhythm, simply by speaking those words. Others
who have no speech may well have some sense of rhythm which
they can express with a part of their bodies. Thus, the use of
rhythm, however simple, becomes another basis for musical
activity with our children.

A. E. Tansley,[1] who has initiated much original work with
neurologically impaired children, believes that there is a strong
connection between rhythmic ability and reading ability.
Exactly how this connection functions is not clear, but we can
expect that experience in rhythmic work will help children to
become generally more fluent and co-ordinated, thereby gaining
confidence in such activities as reading and language use in
which fluency most certainly helps.

In the music sessions we can encourage the children to play
and speak the words of simple rhymes. This can be done in a
variety of ways, by combining together playing and speaking,
or by speaking the rhymes over a clear pulse. Sometimes different
rhythms can be combined over a common pulse to give interesting cross-rhythmic effects. This needs careful control by all
concerned; also, it is wise to give the different rhythmic patterns

to clearly contrasted percussive groups:

Step 1   All the children say the verse, then clap its rhythm

     2   Drummers clap, then play line 2

     3   Wood-block players clap, then play line 2

     4   Tambourines clap, then play line 3

     5   Maracas clap, then play line 4

     6   Perform the whole verse, each group of instruments playing its own line in turn

     7   Drummers repeat their line many times; each of the other groups plays its own rhythm to make cross-rhythms with the drummers

     8   Combine any lines ad libitum

The children enjoy having their own names tapped, clapped, or played as rhythms. This can be initiated as a game or it can be used as an excellent introduction to a lesson; using their names has the additional advantage of making them feel important as individuals. Sometimes it is useful to include the rhythms of some of their names on a prepared tape which includes other listening material. If they are told that their own names are somewhere in the taped programme they will be motivated to listen more intently. Other material on the tape might include sounds of the instruments, their own compositions, songs, and sounds which belong to a series of events, i.e. a simple story in sound. This might involve footsteps, a closing door, a car starting and driving away, a bucket being picked up and filled with water, a kettle boiling, a ball bouncing, bird song, trains, etc. Most modern cassette recorders are quite adequate for collecting realistic outdoor sounds. The children can be asked to judge the age of the person who is walking, or the state of the weather, or the time of day from the sounds they hear. This is an extremely good aural exercise as well as a means of extending the imaginative processes of the children, and some of them are so good at recognising certain sounds that they can identify the actual makes of motor cars.

The tape recorder may be used to reinforce a study of everyday rhythms. Try to find out and record, with the children, all the things which use a regular pulse or rhythm, e.g. clocks, carpenters, the human heart, people walking and running, engines, etc. Some of these can be imitated by the children with their instruments, and they might explore very simple ways of writing down the rhythms they hear. The difference between a walking and a running pulse could be:

$$\text{walking} \quad - \; - \; - \; - \; - \; - \; - \; -$$
$$\text{running} \quad .. \; .. \; .. \; .. \; .. \; .. \; ..$$

Simple word rhythms can help the children to compose tunes on the xylophones and glockenspiels. Teachers who use Orff techniques often begin by playing these rhythms on just two notes—G and E (the notes which belong to the lowest lines of the treble clef). This distinctive interval is a minor third, and it is reminiscent of the cuckoo and of the musical sound which children tend to use in the playground when calling to each other. The children will quickly wish to progress to using other notes, and it is at this point that a pentatonic scale can be provided for them to explore. It is possible to build up towards using the pentatonic scale very gradually, e.g.:

Step 1   using G and E   Step 2   using G, E, and A
Step 3   G, E, A, and D   Step 4   G, E, A, D, and C

Teachers should understand that the resulting melodies and the implied harmony of these various groups of notes do not belong firmly to a *key*. For example, at step 3, an invented melody

may come to a close on any of the notes—G E A or D, and those
of us who have been steeped in music which is harmonically
based will tend to feel that the melodies belong to G major,
E minor, D major or minor, and so on. There is a strong argument
against such harmonic interpretations, which is quite valid but
which need not demand our attention here. What can be severely
limiting is the idea that there is only one pentatonic scale which
is rooted on C, so that all the work which is done sounds as if
the players are limited by a diatonic scale of C major with some
notes missing! Anyone who studies folk melodies will realise
that the majority of them do not belong firmly to a particular
key and its implied primary chords. These melodies are often
described as *modal*, and as such are very self-sufficient; if they
do imply any particular harmonies, this is incidental.

    Let us consider the pentatonic scale G A B D E, which sounds:
doh ray me — soh lah — (doh'). This scale has no semitones.
A pentatonic scale can also be formed from the notes C D E G A,
or F G A C D, or in many other ways, including the use of the
five black keys on the piano. Because it has no semitones, it is
difficult to make strongly discordant sounds when the notes are
played in harmony. The pentatonic scale lends itself well to
melodic improvisation. The teacher will realize that a good
many folk tunes from all over the world, and particularly from
Asia, where Orff became fascinated by its extensive use, are
made from it. Let the children explore the scale freely; owing
to its pleasant harmonic implications, it will allow a number of
improvisors to play at once without causing distress to the
onlookers and listeners. Some children will be pleased to discover
that they can pick out parts of recognizable tunes—'The Skye
boat song', 'Swing low, sweet chariot', 'Auld lang syne' are all
examples of pentatonic tunes. If there is a music corner in the
classroom, snippets of tunes can be written out for the children
to play in odd moments. As a first step, the letter names of the
notes may be used but we know that many slow learning
children can cope with staff notation as long as the examples
are short and written out very clearly and as large as possible.

    Melodic improvisation can be organized as a very enjoyable
group activity. Provide as many of the children as possible with

xylophones, glockenspiels, or chime bars. Arrange all the bars so that each child has access to the notes CDE GA (or whichever pentatonic scale the teacher prefers). If some players can have notes which extend beyond the close range—CDE GA—to give them G_1A_1 CDE GA C^1, all the better. Few schools will have the complete array of instruments which Orff specialists prefer, but it is possible for the children to work in pairs, taking turns if necessary, in order to involve more participants. Select a child who can maintain a steady pulse and teach him to play an ostinato or repeated figure, preferably on the bass xylophone. A simple drone, using the lowest C together with the next G above, will provide an excellent ground bass over which the other barred instruments may improvise.

This drone needs to be repeated over and over again, as if it were a repeated minim at a speed of about MM 86. The children who improvise will need to play their melodies mainly as crotchets, but will be encouraged to include whatever rhythmic patterns they discover. Help them to feel the pulse so that they keep together by playing in neat sequences of four, eight or sixteen bars each. A good structure for this improvisation is a rondo form. For the 'chorus' of the rondo, let all the children play. Each one may then try to play a solo in turn, sandwiched between the choruses; remember that the bass player keeps the 'obstinate' drone going through the entire improvisation. If the children tend to accelerate, the teacher might play a gentle pulse on a tambour tuned to C or G.

As well as improvisation, group compositions can be worked out by choosing short verbal phrases to which simple tunes are added. Some teachers like to use words connected with a particular topic, such as *food* which involves phrases like 'fish and chips', 'steak and kidney pudding', 'apple pie and custard'. Individuals or groups can rehearse their phrases, having set them to simple pentatonic tunes, and the various phrases may then be added together, over an ostinato if required.

The possibilities of combining word rhythms and pentatonic melodies are endless. Try working with different pulse measures, at different speeds, and in different forms. Explore the effect of combining the various barred instruments in terms of counterpoint, pitch and tonal colour, and add untuned percussive rhythms and punctuations from time to time.

Certain children discover abilities they were not previously aware of when they are encouraged to improvise; this is especially true where melodic improvisation is concerned. The greater the variety of activities we offer them, the more likely it is that they will discover something they feel they can do well.

Melodic instruments

Some of the slow-learning children are able to make reasonable progress on recorders and melodicas. There is no way of judging their aptitude and readiness, apart from giving them an opportunity to try the instruments, but the perceptive teacher will be able to decide if and when regular and positive teaching is to be initiated. Novel systems of teaching and notation have been tried in a number of schools, using colours, dots, and other visual patterns to represent fingering, but most teachers resort to the use of letter names, or a combination of staff notation and letter names. In the author's experience, letter names can be dispensed with quite quickly and the ordinary staff notation eventually used without resort to any other aids. It is essential, as with any group of musicians, to present the children with musical notation which is as neat and clear as possible, and most players find large and well spaced notation easier to read than small, cramped print. There is no reason why hand-printed notation should not be as clear as, or even clearer than, commercially produced material.

Most ESN children who play recorders do not begin learning seriously until the age of about eleven years. There are a number of physical, perceptual, and conceptual processes which must mature before the various co-ordinations needed for playing are possible. Fine finger control, breathing, rhythmic and pitch abilities, and an overall understanding of what is required, must all be present to ensure that a start can be made. Usually the children begin by learning to play G, A, and B on the descant recorders, and then work gradually upwards and downwards from those notes. Encourage beginners to blow gently downwards into the instruments, making a 'too' sound for each note to give it precision of attack. Use a variety of approaches, sometimes holding an instrument in front of them and showing the finger patterns for easy phrases, sometimes playing the phrases as they watch the notation and finger the holes without blowing. Ensure that the children have plenty of opportunities to see and hear the teacher play their phrases for them. They need much repetition of the sounds and patterns if they are to imitate and eventually produce musically satisfying results.

School recorder books are mostly excellently graded and well founded on experience with child learners. The tunes these books contain, however, soon become tiresome, especially to teachers who have introduced several groups of beginners to the instrument. Unfortunately the small range of notes which are within the scope of beginners seriously limits the choice of tunes in existence, but there is no reason why the teacher should not write original simple tunes for them. Sometimes, too, there are currently popular jingles and phrases of pop tunes which are remarkably simple and which can serve as recorder playing material. In the early 1970s such tunes as 'Amazing grace', 'I'd like to teach the world to sing', and 'Eye Level' found their way into many school recorder concerts. The latter tune might have been written especially for school recorders, as the whole theme lay within the compass of seven notes and contained mainly stepwise phrases. Very simple tunes using only three or four notes can be made more interesting by the addition of a rich harmonic or rhythmically stimulating accompaniment, thus satisfying the need of the children to play some 'real' music. This is quite musically valid; one of the best known of Bach's chorale settings, 'Jesu, joy of man's desiring', is based on only seven adjacent notes.

It is wise to teach F sharp—rather than F natural—early on, and then introduce C sharp, so that an octave from D to D is quickly built up. The low C on descant recorders is quite difficult as it needs good, gentle breath control, which comes only after practice on the higher notes. Within this octave, D to D, there are many tunes available; most of them will be found in recorder books, but it also gives an imaginative teacher very good scope for writing new tunes. For useful idioms and forms on which to base these compositions, look to present day sources, e.g. popular dance rhythms—particularly those of Latin America—tunes from musical shows, TV themes and modern hymns. The key of D is particularly useful to work within because it offers the possibility of adding guitar chords, and open string accompaniment on most of the stringed instruments, and is convenient for many of the songs we need to pitch fairly low for our singers.

Some schools have made very good use of melodicas.[2] There seem to be no established techniques for fingering and holding these interesting instruments; it is very much a matter of trial and error. Generally, the bigger and more expensive melodicas produce a more pleasant sound than the smallest models. A distinct advantage with these instruments is that well tuned notes at the extremes of the range are no more difficult to produce than those in the middle register. Also, chords are possible! The recorder parts can be simply duplicated on the melodicas; this is a useful time-saver for the teacher.

Most beginners on recorders, and orchestral instruments in general, make sounds in their practice periods which are disturbing to their neighbours. Ways might have to be found for some of our children to practise privately at school, especially where the children's homes are not conducive or encouraging to music-making. Recorder beginners in particular must be strongly discouraged from over-blowing and making shrieks; damage to the instrument, and possibly to the ear, can result from this practice. To many, school recorder playing is not a very satisfying musical experience owing to the limitations of the instrument and of the players (except in the case of a few brilliant performers—but these are rare). I feel, however, that the advantages offered by these instruments strongly outweigh the disadvantages, and that new musical avenues can be opened through playing them. For some brighter children, the recorder is an excellent preparatory instrument for later experience on the clarinet, oboe, and flute. For our children it may be an additional way of training the ear, gaining a wider understanding of melody, exercising the lungs, and above all providing another means of participating in music-making with others.

Movement

When we considered activities for the younger ESN children,
the point was made that music and movement are so closely
allied that it is difficult to engage in one without the other.
Young children normally sing, move, and dance quite spon-
taneously, and many teachers wonder what happens later on
when this natural activity seems to become lost. This is even more
puzzling when the very noticeable trend for modern musicians,
both 'serious' and popular, is towards the involvement of movement, dance, and drama in their musical performances. The fact
is that our bodies enjoy functioning as instruments; they are
themselves expressive in very similar ways to the instruments
of music. Within our bodies we can experience variations of
speed, rhythm, growth, shape, and form. Often, a greater understanding of and feeling for certain pieces of music come out of
the movement and dance we do to it.

Perhaps we do not ensure continuity and integration of the
various aspects of the musical art in our schools. We do know
that the group of children we have in mind in this chapter can
gain enormous benefits through movement, not only as a way
of enriching their musical experience, but also as an additional
means of furthering their physical and emotional growth. The
following activities are suggested as starting points, in the hope
that the teacher will see further possibilities and become
interested enough to take courses in movement and study the
available literature.

A reasonable space is necessary. It should have a clean, warm
floor which is free from splinters, a power point for a small
portable record player, and a small table on which a few percussion instruments can be placed. The children need to be
suitably clothed for movement; 'P.E.' clothes are fine and if
possible, the children should be encouraged to move in their
bare feet.

Our pupils in particular will need plenty of time to discover
just what their bodies can do. An early aim will be to encourage
an awareness of their bodies. Teachers new to this work will be
surprised to find that some children need reminding where their

elbows, shoulders, ankles, and heels are! Use the tambour to establish pulses for walking, running, striding, shuffling, and hopping. Tell them which parts of themselves they must concentrate on whilst they are moving, e.g. 'think about your toes', 'press your heels into the ground', 'make patterns in the air with your knees'. Do not be afraid to demonstrate the kinds of movements you want them to make. They need to imitate for much longer periods than normal children.

Use the percussion instruments to help them make movements of different qualities. In the music sessions, the cymbal played long, slow sounds. Now, in the bigger space, they can make long slow movements. It may be necessary to suggest that they are trying to escape from a sticky environment. The shaking instruments may suggest shaking movements, or quick running steps. To a crescendo, they will probably enjoy growing from a low crouching position to a high stretched position, or they might open out from a curled up position. If the teacher stands in the middle of the room and plays a crescendo on the tambour, they can approach slowly, in a menacing way. Concentrate on opposites, which are useful concepts to learn. The opposite to crescendo is diminuendo, and to sounds which decrease in volume they may shrink from a high to a low position, or curl up from an open position. To loud sounds they will make large, energetic movements; to soft sounds small, light movements. Use a small glockenspiel to play ascending and descending scales. Even children who show confusion between high and low sounds get the feeling of gradually rising and falling to a moving scale passage.

The degree of control the teacher has over the children's instrumental playing, and the control they have over their instruments can both be reinforced if some of the sound games already described are played in the large space of the movement room. Further work on locating the source and direction of quiet sounds can be done now, using greater distances to extend the children's concentration. 'Statues' is a useful game for reinforcing control, stimulating alertness, and encouraging the children to concentrate their attention carefully. The game may be played in two main ways, with the teacher as the mover or with

the teacher as the instrumentalist. The basic idea is extremely
simple. Give each child a small percussion instrument and the
instruction, 'you only make sounds with the instruments when
I move'. At first, make the movements expansive and the
'statues' clearly posed. Thus, it will be obvious to the children
when they should both play and stop playing. Gradually change
to making finer and smaller movements so that their concentration
is focused on the hands, feet, fingers, toes, eyes, and even eye-
brows. If the teacher moves into a position where only certain
players can see her face, she can, with a hand behind her back,
demand sounds from various groups of players and even devise
a short sound composition in the process. The second way to
play the game is for the teacher to use an instrument which
dictates, by sounding and stopping frequently, when the children
should move, and when they should make their statue poses.
Again, increase the demands made on the children by playing
fairly loudly in the early stages so that the silences are strongly
contrasted, then by choosing a quiet instrument on which very
soft sounds are made later on.

Use the movement sessions to introduce country dancing.
If the teacher is unfamiliar with a number of traditional dances,
these can be easily learnt from books of instructions, but it is
perhaps better to devise simple dances to suit the abilities of the
particular children in the class. Remember that sequences are
invariably in eights, which makes for ease of invention and
control of the steps the children are asked to do. Almost any
standard recording[3] of country dance tunes will do. A simple
dance to 'Brighton camp' ('The girl I left behind me') could be
as follows:
The children form a circle, or two circles if more convenient,
and locate their partners (who are standing next to them).
1, eight steps in a clockwise direction; 2, eight steps anti-
clockwise; 3, eight steps into the middle; 4, eight steps back;
5, promenade (walk side by side) with partners, eight steps
clockwise; 6, promenade eight steps anti-clockwise; 7, clap
eight times, facing the centre of the circle; 8, swing partners to
a count of eight.
In a number of ESN schools, country dancing is taken to a high

degree of skill and complexity. Apart from the more obvious
benefits of this kind of dancing, which gives the children a sense
of sequence, form, and patterning, some children are helped to
come to terms with their spatial problems and to learn which is
their right and left side (!), and how to participate sensibly with
the opposite sex.

In her collection of recordings on disc and tape, the teacher
will be wise to include short pieces which might be used to
stimulate a variety of movements and dances. Some of these will
be light and popular and useful for walking, skipping, swaying,
and even resting. Other music will suggest moods which help
the children to imagine themselves in the kind of situations
already suggested. By moving to music and by 'living' it in
pretence situations, they will gain a deep experience of it.

The relationship of music to other activities

It is hoped that the children will continue to have visiting
musicians as they did in the reception class, and as they get
older we can make more demands on their capacity to listen
and to remember the correct names of the instruments and
what the pieces are about. Follow-up work is essential. Tape
recordings, drawings, and pieces of writing need to be done and
displayed. By now, some of the children may be taken out to
performances of music for schools.

Drawing, writing, and reading activities can be associated
with the music the children hear on record and tape as well as
the live performances. In an experiment in one school, the
children made extremely interesting verbal and pictorial
responses to a variety of music which included some modern
jazz, the Fantasia on a theme of Thomas Tallis, by Vaughan
Williams, some classical Indian sitar music, and a Bach bourrée
played by Segovia. One child imagined a 'giraffe drinking water',
another visualised an Eastern bazaar for the Indian music, and
several made grotesque pictures for the Vaughan Williams
Fantasia. Many of their ideas could be directly traced to the
influence of television, and this was considered no bad thing;
at least some vicarious experience had been memorized and

appropriately recalled as a result of the musical stimulus in the classroom.

There may be opportunities for the children to provide musical effects for puppet plays, dramatic activities, and the school pantomime. A later chapter will include a discussion of the relationship of music to the whole school, but it seems necessary here to stress the importance of extending music beyond the walls of the classroom (or music room if the school is lucky enough to have one). Every opportunity should be taken to perform to other class groups; the daily act of worship provides a splendid opportunity to do this and it can have the effect of bringing to life what is often a boring and meaningless occasion.

For further suggestions about the ways in which music can be linked with other school activities, see *The Slow Learner and Music*, by J. P. B. Dobbs (Oxford University Press).

Music teachers have an advantage over their colleagues in that they have at their fingertips a variety of exciting resources which they can use as aids to communication and closer relationships with the children. The music teacher can be a very interesting person who often brings new instruments and performers to the school and who is possibly a skilled performer herself. Slow-learning children are frequently very proud of their teacher's musicianship; one often hears the remark, 'You should be on the telly, Miss!' when music is played expertly to them. After all, it is the relationship between teacher and children which counts most highly and it is likely that the activities with 'our music teacher' will be remembered by the children much longer than some of the more functional activities.

Notes

[1] A. E. Tansley *Reading and remedial reading* Routledge and Kegan Pau
[2] These hybrid instruments generate the sounds with mouth organ reeds, which are exposed and closed to the blown air stream by means of a conventional keyboard.
[3] See Appendix II

4   Music for older slow-learning children

The suggestions in the following chapter are based on activities
observed and tried out with ESN children of at least thirteen
years of age and with children in secondary school special classes,
often known as remedial classes. Secondary school teachers who
read these suggestions need to realise that the smallness of the
special schools makes for flexibility of time-tables and available
spaces and varied groupings of the children, all of which can be
used to great advantage where music activity is concerned. The
limitations of working within 40 minute modules, which tends
to be the pattern in many large secondary schools, are fully
recognized, but it is hoped that the reader who has to work
within such a pattern will find the descriptions of the actual
activities helpful.

The organization of music groups

Many of the best activities are done at times which are quite
outside the set music periods. In one school, the music teacher
was given a day each week when she was encouraged to select
any individuals and small groups from the senior ESN classes
which she considered might benefit from or make good progress
in music activities. In another school, the use of lunch-time
periods and an afternoon each week which was devoted to
'club'—i.e. free choice—activities allowed for groupings of
children according to aptitude and interest. Consequently,
faster progress was made with these groups formed on the basis
of musical ability and interest than would have been possible
with the chronological class group.

I feel that far too little thought is given in many schools to
the way children are grouped for their various activities. The
common practice of grouping according to chronological age is
clearly convenient for organizational reasons, and it does have
the advantage of pinpointing milestones of maturity, i.e. going
'up' to the next class, but there is much to be gained from
'setting' according to the activity especially where music is

concerned. In the senior part of the school, the children begin
to realise their relatively special abilities and interests, and they
need plenty of opportunities to work with friends who share
those interests and who can stimulate them to make good
progress in the activity. In those schools where this method of
grouping according to activity is widely practised, the standards
achieved by the children are usually very high. Music, movement, physical education, art, and motor mechanics are all
activities observed in ESN schools in which standards
equivalent to any normal secondary school can be attained.

The school choir

A selected choir is one excellent way of grouping the children
to ensure a good standard of performance. There is something
to be gained from 'auditioning' children before they are
admitted. This makes the point at the outset that a good
standard is expected, but the teacher will need to be sensitive
to those children whose voices are not secure if they are
especially sincere in their wish to join the choir. It is recognised
that a successful choir, with its implied privileges, e.g. going out
to sing at concerts and other events, may attract members who
wish to join for the 'wrong' reasons. Only the teacher, perhaps
with the head-teacher's help, can judge where the line is to be
drawn. As with the younger classes, the children in the choir
should be encouraged to sing with vitality and to make full use
of the lower range of their voices. Later on, when part-singing
is attempted, this rich lower range will add greatly to the distinctive sound which ESN choirs can make. Beware of the
danger of staying too long in this range; many of the children
are also quite capable of being extended vocally into the high
register involving a clear top G (next to the fifth line of the
treble clef). Teachers who start out with expectations of success
are likely to achieve it, and occasionally one finds that choir
trainers who are quite inexperienced with ESN children are able
to get remarkable results, because they have no preconceptions
about the children's abilities. It will be desirable to choose
material which lends itself to vigorous singing—again American

folk songs, certain popular songs, spirituals, modern hymns, and songs from musical shows are all good sources.

The problem of learning words may be dismissed at once. Certainly, ESN children have not the facility to pick up a song copy and immediately read the music and the words. Generally speaking, the use of individual copies of words and music is not a good idea for these children. They will, however, be greatly helped by having the words displayed on a large card, as for the younger children, and the music teacher should take care to use the orthography which is most commonly accepted in the school. Secure the card in a fairly high position in order to encourage the children to project their voices 'upwards'; the children's attention can be focused on any particular words or climaxes which need extra care by pointing to them. A later step can be the provision of well-spaced typed word-sheets; the children can proudly keep these in a folder, which will be useful if and when the choir travels to perform. There is hardly any limitation to the number of words the children can cope with, provided that the vocabulary is relevant to their experience and efficiently taught. More than one ESN choir has been known to perform songs from musical shows involving as many as 1500 words (at one performance), which were mostly memorised. For these choirs, the teaching involved many regular practices with rote learning, line by line and phrase by phrase. This was sometimes reinforced by playing professional and home-made recordings of the songs, but the learning was usually accomplished within the space of one school term. When intensive learning sessions are planned, it is helpful to have a second person available to play the accompaniment or to point to the words as they are being followed by the children, but it is realised that this is not always possible. Sometimes a good reader from the choir can be invited to point. A list of suggested songs and musical plays is included in Appendix II, but the following material is especially recommended for the school choir:

Joseph and the Amazing Technicolor Dreamcoat, by T. Rice and A. Lloyd-Webber (Novello); songs from *Jesus Christ*, *Superstar* by the same composers (Leeds Music); songs from *Chitty Chitty Bang Bang*, *Oliver*, and *The sound of music*, with melody and

words and with reasonably simplified accompaniments (Chappell);
'Kumbayah' and 'Thank you' from *Faith, Folk and Clarity*
(Galliard); *Jonah Man Jazz* by Michael Hurd (Novello); *The battle
of Elah* (David and Goliath) and *Go Moses*, by David Ward (single
copies only available from the composer at Dartington College
of Arts).

Two-part singing is well within the scope of many ESN school
choirs, but this is not necessarily preferable to good unison
singing. Many rounds can be sung as a means of introducing part
singing, although it cannot be assumed that the singing of rounds
will automatically lead into part singing. Some ESN choirs learn
the descants and second parts as tunes in their own right and
only later on add them to the main melody of the song. In one
school, the choir made good use of a commercial recording as a
model for part singing. Unfortunately there is very little published
material to meet this particular need, and teachers are encouraged
to write their own simple second parts and descants to suit the
abilities of their particular children. It is not difficult to devise a
simple descant based on the implied harmony of certain songs.
The following descant to 'Kumbayah' has been effectively used
with ESN children:

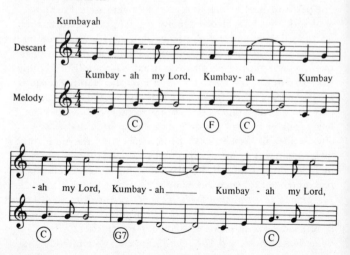

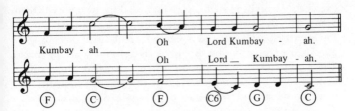

This easy second part to 'What shall we do with the drunken sailor' was used with the same children:

Chorus - 'What shall we do with the drunken sailor?'

The discovery of harmony in choral work is one of the most exciting and satisfying events in the whole of musical activity. It goes without saying that the children need to realise that their different vocal parts are complementary, and not competitive as in the party game where one group attempts to sing louder than another!

Some consideration should be given to the space in which the choir performs and rehearses. Plenty of reverberation (echo) can add greatly to the singing by giving it a feeling of expansiveness, but during early rehearsals too much reverberation can amplify extraneous sounds in such a way that teaching becomes difficult. Sometimes the speed of a performance has to be adjusted to suit the acoustic peculiarities of a particular hall. In all our music-making, careful attention should be given to the working spaces. There is usually little choice, but often a change of room will make a considerable improvement to the sounds which are being produced and to the ease of control and organization of the session.

How many singers should there be in the school choir? Smaller special schools sometimes involve the entire school in the choir, and this has the advantage of initiating the youngest children into what is, to them, a tradition. Obviously, the size of the school and the aptitudes of the children will determine the size of any musical group; most ESN choirs have from 25– 30 members, and this seems a convenient size to ensure a full sound without bringing with it the complications of handling very large numbers of children and too wide a range of vocal ability and maturity. If the older boys' interest is captured early enough and if the choir is conducted in a business-like and exciting way, their vocal contributions can add greatly to the sound the choir makes, even when their voices begin to change. I remember one 15-year-old boy, in particular, who had a haunting counter-tenor voice which would have delighted many great choir trainers. Quite often, our slow learning children are surprisingly uninhibited about singing solo verses of the songs we introduce. Wherever possible, these soloists should be encouraged to use their voices and enjoy the feeling of per-forming to others. School may be the only place where they are recognised for their worth and, because voices change, many of them may have only a few precious years in which to exploit this ability.

Instrumental work

Where instrumental work is concerned, it seems even more necessary to organise activities according to musical abilities rather than on the basis of chronological age or intelligence levels. By the time they reach the senior stage in school, their aptitudes for playing instruments will be emerging. Some will be especially facile with drumming and other percussive activities, some will tend towards the playing of wind instruments. Orchestral instruments, particularly the brass family, are well within the capabilities of some ESN children. There is one group presently well-known in England for its brass playing. The fifteen boys who belong to this group have the rare opportunity of learning under an experienced band instructor who makes few concessions to their limitations of basic skills in reading and reasoning. As far as can be ascertained, they are taught to play their cornets, trombones, and horns quite straightforwardly in regular individual and group music lessons; many of them take the Associated Board grades. They approach the whole business of band work in a professional way, wearing simple uniform, using attractive music stands, and playing from ordinary commercially produced band parts. The sound they make is comparable with any English small town band.

To be realistic, not many schools can offer such expertise of teaching, and the necessary resources to attain the high standards of performance of this group. But the music advisers and tutorial staff of local education authorities might bear in mind the proved capabilities of some ESN children, when making provision for the children in their areas. The benefits, to our children in particular, of playing in bands are so obvious that they need not be stated.

Earlier in this chapter a school was mentioned which gave its music teacher complete freedom to select and work with any individuals and groups for a whole day each week. In this school, a small orchestra was formed with four melodicas, three xylophone and glockenspiel players, one 'jazz' drummer (a mongol boy), and several other children who played untuned percussion instruments. They played arrangements of popular tunes such as the *Z-Cars* theme, and a medley of sea songs written and performed for a special occasion. Some of the tunes in this medley modulated smartly through various keys, including F sharp major, and careful attention had been paid to clarity and interest in the tonal combination of instruments. In another school, where individual and sectional teaching was also the order of the day, there was a larger orchestra of 12 recorder players, a rhythm section, a jazz drummer, electric organ and stylophone[1], and two electric guitar players. These children, in contrast to those in the smaller orchestra who learned their music by rote, had been trained to use simple orchestrations involving a combination of letter names and staff notation. Their ability to cope at first sight with a new arrangement—although this was very simple— was quite remarkable. Another similar school orchestra of severely sub-normal children performed so well that I thought that a group of teachers must be playing as I listened outside the music room. Here again, no teaching gimmicks or novel methods were apparently used; just plain, straightforward approaches. They had, earlier on, been taught correct beater techniques for the playing of xylophones and glockenspiels, and apart from large, clearly printed 'orchestrations' and a well equipped music room they were no more especially advantaged than any other school.

It seems that reasonable facilities, good organization, a high level of expectation, optimism, and much hard work by an enthusiastic teacher can produce very good musical results with children who might be otherwise very limited in their ability to learn. A supportive head-teacher and opportunities for performing to others are also necessary for the continuation of good results. It is quite clear to anyone who observes these performances that the children themselves realise their own levels of success and gain a significant sense of achievement which must surely transfer to other areas and contribute considerably to their developing personalities.

In a very tough London school the teacher conducted a courageous experiment based on the idea that children need much freedom to explore the possibilities of musical instruments before they can begin to learn exact techniques of playing. The ESN boys who came to the music room—a spare cloakroom— were boisterous and often quite aggressive, but the teacher was convinced that given freedom to play how they liked—and this often meant very loudly—they would eventually feel the need for variety and for some constructive teaching. This group was observed at the beginning of the experiment, and again six

months later. It was quite remarkable how their musicianship
had developed. During the later observational visit, when the
boys were engaged in 'musical conversations' (see page 23) they
played their contributions most sensitively and imaginatively.
Most had settled down to enjoy studying simple techniques of
playing; the group feeling had changed from aggressive chaos
to gentle control. The therapeutic value of music activities was
clearly highlighted.

Whilst the older children enjoy creating simple compositions
and improvisations in sound—and some of them may need taking
back over the earlier stages of awareness and discrimination of
sounds as described in chapter II—they also feel the need to make
music which sounds like the music of their everyday lives.
In this popular music there is a very simple component which
lends itself to a variety of instantly successful activities; this is
harmonic structure. Western popular music in the first half of
the present century was largely influenced by jazz, which
originated in the blues. The blues somehow served to satisfy a
basic need of the negroes, who had been so oppressed by slavery
in America during the last century. A typical blues sequence has
a neat twelve-bar chord progression, thus:

line 1   four bars—tonic chord, or doh + me + soh
   2   two bars —subdominant chords, or fah + lah + doh
   3   two bars —tonic chord
   4   two bars —dominant chord, or soh + te + ray
   5   two bars —tonic chord.

All these chords may have an additional minor seventh added—
e.g. tonic chord + taw, subdominant chord + maw, dominant
chord + fah.

Our children find this, and other simple, orderly chord
sequences easy and satisfying to work with. Guitars, autoharps,
chime bars, xylophones, glockenspiels, the piano, string bass or
tea-chest bass, mouth-organs, and melodicas can all be used to
play chords or some of the notes which make up the chords.
Begin in a very simple way by organizing a group of children,
each of whom has a chime bar which belongs to the chord of
D major, i.e. D, F sharp, and A. Let them play together on a
steady pulse, so that they can enjoy and appreciate the pleasing

sound the chord makes. Play this same D major chord on the guitar or autoharp, tuned to the chime bars, to demonstrate that individual notes join together to make a chord. Organize another group who play chime bars belonging to the A major chord, i.e. A, C sharp, and E, and make a similar comparison with the guitar and autoharp. Now plan a simple sequence which uses these chords and to which a well-known tune can be sung or played, e.g.

'He's got the whole world in his hand'

This system of notation for chord playing will be familiar to guitarists; a comparison with the staff notation may help to make it clear:

Other tunes which use just two chords can be performed in a similar way. Examples of these are: 'Tom Dooley', 'Pick a bale o' cotton', 'Lord of the dance', and the verses only of 'Oh, Susannah' and 'The Camptown races'.

Songs with three or more chords can now be attempted. Children who have instruments with a complete chromatic scale, e.g. melodicas, some xylophones, and glockenspiels, can be encouraged to play various combinations of the notes of the appropriate chords and to work out suitable patterns for the style and rhythm of the tunes which are being accompanied. Some schools have used this sort of harmonic work as a basis for their own compositions of popular and folk-style songs.

One large secondary school for girls has an annual folk-song festival which includes a competition to write and perform an original 'folk-song'. Most of these compositions are very much tied to the easier guitar chords. The less able children in this school take part on equal terms with the other children.

The organization of music activities with any group involves making the very best use of the abilities of the participants, devising group activities which make reasonable demands on the players, planning individual and group instruction and rehearsals carefully, making good use of the physical resources available, and encouraging the musicians to work towards the very best performance they are capable of giving. The teacher's own musical abilities, confidence, taste, enthusiasm, and love for music are all factors which affect the day to day activities. Also, her ability to make good relationships with her colleagues is of vital importance if the music activities are to enrich the entire life of the school. All-round relationships with people and with topics must be made, to ensure that music is not a self-conscious or isolated subject which only exists in order to perpetuate itself, or as the province of a privileged minority.

Music teachers do not always realise what enormous possibilities they have for stimulating the work of the whole school, and particularly the day-to-day work of their colleagues. It is interesting to note that in some sub-normality hospitals, the introduction of a lively music therapist has on more than one occasion helped to boost the morale of the staff. On festive occasions, or indeed at any time when the school assembles together, there must be music. Sometimes, teacher colleagues who appear to be musically indifferent can be persuaded to co-operate in a variety of ways—perhaps by producing scenery or the script or dialogue for a musical play or pantomime. One teacher whose regular disapproval of the choice of music for the daily act of worship gave him the reputation of being 'anti-musical' became one of the most exciting contributors when asked to present music of his own choice. Through the teachers' active participation in plays and pantomimes (some of them enjoy dressing up in a comical role!) new relationships with the children are made and a sense of fun can be injected into the whole school's activity. On these occasions, the choir, recorder group, band, and percussion section can all be combined to work towards a splendid performance.

Music festivals

Some school music festival committees make an extra effort to involve children from special schools in their activities. One group of physically handicapped recorder players frequently won prizes in their county's competitive festival; no concessions were made by the adjudicators for their handicap. In noncompetitive festivals, there is always the possibility of including simple items which suit the capabilities of the slow learning participants, but often our children discover, much to their delight, that they can take part on equal terms with the other children. On more than one occasion, they have been able to project a special feeling of vitality into songs by their unselfconscious and strongly rhythmic singing and playing.

Although it is good to observe the happy integration of special and normal groups in these festivals, there are certain advantages to be gained from the joining together of special schools in their own music festivals. One school can often stimulate the work of another; sometimes teachers who are modest about their children's achievements are reassured when they compare them with those of other schools. Festivals, and other occasions which demand the best possible performances, can do much to motivate the children's activities, to make the sharing of ideas and repertoire possible, and to give that general feeling of exhilaration created by massed performances.

Classroom work in music

So far, the suggestions in this chapter have been made on the basis that music groups of varying sizes can be organized during the school day, ideally fitting into the existing system of class and timetable organization in the school. In certain situations, this may not be possible, and the music teacher may have to teach classes which have been formed mainly on the basis of chronological age. In this situation, unfortunately, individual lessons and specific group activities have to take place in the lunch break; unless the school is residential the children will not have opportunities for after-school activities. Music teachers often find that these lunch-time sessions do not lend themselves to a serious enough approach on the part of the children; they feel somehow that activities which are done in 'free' time are not as important as those which are timetabled. With older classes, music activities tend to become difficult in any case, and, for a variety of reasons the children may not want to do music any longer. When this happens it is helpful to broaden the scope of the activities offered, and to look for additional associated work which might appeal more to those who are disenchanted. The following suggestions are based on obser-vations and practical experience of music projects done in several schools where there was, in the older children, a low level of musical motivation.

One teacher initiated a class project which was centred around music, although for much of the time the children did not associate it with 'music lessons'. As a starting point television programmes were studied through discussion and by the collection of *TV* and *Radio Times* cuttings which gave the dates and times of programmes and information about the characters who appeared in the programmes. Work cards for colouring and writing activities were prepared and completed by the children, and quizzes on the programmes were developed and much enjoyed. These quizzes often involved the use of TV signature tunes and concentrated particularly on any musical aspects of the programmes, e.g. the orchestras and band leaders who were employed. The quizzes and work cards gradually began to focus on instruments used by popular and classical musicians. Then the children were asked to take part in a class competition in which points were awarded for any good pictures with musical associations the children could find. Some of them found a surprising number of postage stamps bearing musical motifs. Two whole days were devoted to the making of 'rope-ladder' xylophones from broom handles; the girls took part in this with great enjoyment as they were allowed on this occasion to try their hand in the wood-work room. These xylophones involved accurate measurement of wood and consequent rough-tuning—both activities which demand care, and attention to detail. Three of the more manually able boys extended their interest in instrument-making by working on a parallel project which produced large and durable instruments for an adventure playground. Towards the end of the whole class project a group quiz and individual tests were devised, which required the children to recognise a variety of sounds, including those made by orchestral instruments, on a prepared tape. They were also given a test of their ability to read many of the words they had met on the work-cards and in the quizzes. The results of these tests were very encouraging; apart from the interest which had been stimulated in music, the gain in reading and general knowledge was significant.

Another class was involved in the making of shadow puppets and the subsequent performance of a puppet play. Music was used in this for a background effect. Shadow puppets are easily made from card, cut out in a shape which is distinctive in silhouette. The puppet shapes are mounted on a stick and held close to the back of a white linen screen which must be tightly stretched on a simple frame. The shapes are projected onto the screen by means of a strong light which should be centrally placed behind the puppets and their operators. The children in this class were told the story of a dragon who ravaged local villages and who would only desist when regular sacrifices (of maidens!) were offered. They then decided on the characters and their names. A small, brave boy was selected as the hero who finally subdued the dragon by playing his flute and, to use the children's own phrase, 'killing him with kindness'! Several fight scenes in the play were suitably intensified by noisy drum and cymbal sounds; a simple, charming flute melody was well improvised on a penny whistle by one of the older girls.

Other classes have made short eight-mm cine films to which music was later added and roughly synchronised. Music can easily be taped from radio or records to give special dramatic effects to film sequences, and the children are often surprised at the quite different feeling a musical background gives to a film scene.

The remarkable achievement in film making by one ESN school should be mentioned. Although the children from one particular senior class were mostly responsible for this, the film included scenes which involved almost all the children in the school at some point. To a complete recording of the modern musical *Jesus Christ, Superstar*, short scenes were mimed and filmed 'on location' in the wild parts of the Peak district of England, outside the city's Crown Court, and in local parks and gardens. A quiet Sunday morning had to be chosen for the scene in which Jesus is sentenced by Pilate and subsequently scourged (on the steps of the Court!). Synchronization of acting and sound were achieved by having a skilled tape recorder operator who needed to stop and re-start the machine at various stages. This was a superb production, and the educational benefits to the children were many and varied. The dramatization certainly helped the children to appreciate the whole of this music, and one felt that they understood the story and its significance in a completely new way. Moreover, to capture the whole performance on film and in sound meant that it could be experienced by them more than once.

Movement and dance

For senior ESN girls, movement is especially beneficial. In one school the girls moved with a quality which could not be bettered by children in any school whatever the intelligence range. The teacher appeared to use the minimum of verbal instruction and rarely demonstrated a movement. Often the children were encouraged to imagine themselves in a situation which required them to move in a particular way, e.g. holding an air bubble in the hands and passing it on to another. Good use was also made of objects which move in certain ways or assume interesting shapes. On one occasion, pipe-cleaner shapes were made by the children, placed on the floor, and then copied by their own body shapes. Appropriate music was always played on records, to reinforce the feelings which came with the various movements.

Good use was also made of a few percussion instruments to dictate how and when to move; intensive listening to the sounds was always demanded.

In another school, Scottish country dancing was a flourishing activity for the older boys and girls. The teacher who instructed them was himself an expert in this art and by demonstration he imparted to them a real sense of grace and lightness in the steps, which is a distinctive feature of this kind of dancing. The children were all equipped with kilts and correct shoes; as with the brass group already described, the uniform and 'professional' attitude of the teacher definitely helped to attain a good standard of work. If possible, the children should always dress properly for their activities. For movement, the wearing of leotards is essential if the children are to experience bodily freedom.

In both these schools, it was clear that the movement and dancing had a marked effect upon the way the children moved around the school at all times. They walked with unusual grace and poise and it was the teachers' opinion that a general increase in self-confidence resulted from their activities. In one school where movement was positively taught, the head-teacher believed that it was a main contributing factor of a spurt of reading improvement which happened at the time when the girls were involved in regular movement activity. In other comparable schools, he said, there tended to be a 'plateau' in the graph of reading progress about this same age level.

Notes

[1]   A pocket-sized electric organ played by sliding a stylus over a metal keyboard.

5   Music activities with cerebral palsied children

The observations and descriptions of music activities with cerebral palsied children recorded in the following pages are inevitably subjective, as they relate my own teaching experience over a period of ten years.

Anyone who is involved in musical activity with this particular group of handicapped children starts off with the enormous advantage that they do not need winning over to music; an almost universal love of music is noticeable in them. Live music especially seems to appeal whether they listen to it or make it themselves. An instrumental or vocal solo, well performed, completely relaxes them; they seem to soak up the music like sponges. It is at once moving and fascinating to observe a severely athetoid child completely relaxed when asleep; it is even more moving to witness the soporific effect which music can have on him.

The power of music to communicate can be clearly observed with those cerebral palsied children who have deficiencies of speech. It is reasonable to assume that they find, through producing and listening to musical sounds, a very special satisfaction in communicating in a way which is possible for them. It is probably because of this element of communication that they often function with greater intensity and length of concentration in a musical situation than in many others.

Cerebral palsy affects children in many different ways and to differing degrees; nevertheless, some can be found amongst this group who are remarkably similar. Almost all of these children are able to make some kind of vocal or instrumental sound or to respond in some way to sounds. Given these possibilities, a surprisingly wide variety of activities can be attempted with them.

It may be necessary to tie sleigh bells or to attach beaters to their limbs; only trial and error will enable the teacher to find the most controlled or efficient way to do this. On the whole, gadgets are not recommended, particularly if they are cumbersome, but for some children the only possible way for them to play their sounds might involve the use of a dental stick or headband to which a beater is attached. Given the most efficient bodily movements and simple mechanical resources, some of these children can produce quite complex rhythms on drums and cymbals, and play difficult melodies on the piano, or on xylophones and glockenspiels. Clearly, attention has to be given to the placing and security of the instruments; various hooks, clamps and firm stands for holding the instruments are essential. Philip Bailey provides a fund of such ideas in his book, *They can make music* (Oxford University Press).

Children who are only slightly handicapped can be taught to play recorders, melodicas, the piano, the electric organ, and all the tuned percussion instruments, to a standard which compares well with that of any children. For children with stiff or uncoordinated movements, instrumental work is an excellent way of providing exercise. It is probably wise to enlist the aid of the school physiotherapist, who will appreciate the motivational aspect of the activity and be able to make specific suggestions about the child's posture and physical relationship with the instrument.

In a similar way, singing can be especially helpful to those children who have minor speech and postural defects. Singing demands a special kind of energy, and in working towards a performance the purpose of clear articulation will become obvious. The rhythmic fluency which comes with singing helps the children to use their voices fully, and the emotional release which often occurs when they sing can help to overcome neurological tensions which only add to the embarrassment of speech difficulties when they are made to 'concentrate' on them. In spite of articulation and certain breathing difficulties, cerebral palsied children have singing voices which are as beautiful and flexible as those of normal children.

With few exceptions, all the music activities described in earlier chapters are well within the capabilities of cerebral palsied children. They are especially sensitive to the demands of a performance and almost invariably make tremendous efforts—sometimes at the last minute—to produce their very best when an audience is present. We hesitate to suggest exploiting them and their audiences unfairly, but the demands of 'the day' when the performance is given definitely helps to motivate them to work hard at their musical contributions.

What activities are possible and beneficial for the most severely handicapped children? At concerts and musical plays, they may be given just one or two important sounds to make at the appropriate moment. To some this would appear to be hardly worth the trouble, but for the children it can be of extreme importance. Some of them display great patience in waiting for that important moment when their sound is required. Novel ways may have to be found for them to make these sounds; on one occasion the only way a particular drum effect could be made was by dropping a tennis ball onto the drum head, involving a simple gripping and releasing movement by the player.

Musical improvisation is probably a better way of involving these severely handicapped children. Given that they can all make a sound in one way or another, musical conversations, or 'adoption', or any of the sound games described in chapter 3 are possible. The idea of conversing in sound can be extended and developed if the teacher has some improvising ability on the piano. Use the instrument atonally, or to make a variety of percussive sounds and invite the children to respond to these sounds with their own instruments as if replying to questions. Eye contact is essential with the group as any unnecessary verbal instructions tend to distract from the music. Next, the children might be asked to try to imitate the various piano sounds. A low, percussive cluster of notes can be imitated by a large drum and a widely spread, sustained and dissonant chord can be echoed on a large cymbal. Large percussion instruments which are capable of 'big' sounds are understandably preferred by those children who are handicapped in speech as well as in gross movements. After some exploration of sounds made in the 'conversations' the children will begin to realise that they can be musically expressive within certain limitations. The single, sustained cymbal sounds can vary in intensity; surprisingly peaceful sounds are created by playing this instrument very softly. Busy, loud, drumming sounds express aggression, irritation, or impatience. When the children realise these expressive possibilities and their own capabilities, almost endless improvisations may be attempted. The control and structure which is necessary for this can be provided by the teacher's piano improvisation. Try to establish the idea that the piano's function is to lead the improvisation; then invite the children to join in by making their sounds as and when they feel they are needed. Change the mood often, but always gradually, and try to avoid improvising over a common pulse for too long. This severely limits the possibilities for individual and group rhythmic contributions; variety of rhythm adds an additional dimension to the improvisation.

These group improvisations have been known to continue for as long as fifty minutes with complete involvement of all the participants. Length of performance is not in itself a mark of success, but it does suggest a high level of involvement on the part of the players. These children have so few opportunities to become deeply involved in activity with others. Music certainly makes this possible.

In our school it has proved useful to work towards two productions each year in order to bring together the choir, recorders, percussion group, and any dramatic or narrative elements. The Christmas act of worship involves carols, musical pieces, reading, and simple acting on the nativity theme. Carols need careful choosing and arrangement to suit the range of voice and keys which are convenient for the various players, and often special carols and songs are written to meet the needs and suit the capabilities of the children. Iain Kendell's *Song of Caedmon* and *The Shepherd's Tale* (Chester) have both been performed with few adaptations. The second annual production usually takes place during the summer, at 'open day', and on this occasion *The Midnight Thief* by Richard Rodney Bennett (Belwy Mills Music) and *The Turtle Drum* by Malcolm Arnold (Oxford University Press) have both been performed with actors or puppets. Usually, however, special musical plays are written to involve the choir and various instrumental groups. These speciall-written works are particularly successful as they can be devised with a specific aim in mind, e.g. to teach rhythm through speech or to extend the range of the recorder players.

For certain individual children music activities have clearly beneficial results. The physical exercise involved in playing instruments has already been mentioned, but music seems to offer even greater possibilities where the teaching of basic concepts and the remedial aspects of learning are concerned. Work with long and short sounds can be related to visual representations of those sounds or to a moving pointer or person. Set up two markers about six feet apart in front of the children in a position which they can be easily seen. Invite them to make a continuous instrumental or vocal sound only when you pass between the markers. Place the markers closer together and ask the children what will happen to their continuous sound now. Demonstrate that your moving at different speeds also affects the duration of their sound. The concepts of length, duration, and speed are interestingly related; this relationship sometimes becomes clear to the children when they take part in this kind of activity.

Spatial problems are fairly easy to recognize in these children where their visual and motor abilities are brought into play. We do not know whether some of these brain-injured children have similar problems in the aural field. In the sound games, which require them to locate sounds and judge the distances between the sound source and the ear, we sometimes find that the children make gross errors of judgement. In one of these games, the children are asked to identify and remember three or four locations, well apart in a large room, e.g. the table in the corner, the door, the piano. The children are blindfolded, or placed in such a way that they cannot see these locations, and the teacher moves quietly around the room, making a soft sound with a chime bar, drum, or maraca near each location. The object of the game is to guess where the teacher is standing when the sounds are made. Another activity demanding a similar kind of judgement is a game in which the numerals 1, 2, 3, 4, and 5 are chalked on the floor at intervals of about six feet and in a straight line. The children are positioned either by the number 1 'station' or by number 5, and either blindfolded and facing the numbers, or with their backs to the numbers. The teacher makes a continuous sound as she approaches them by walking *over* the numbers and stops at any station she chooses. The children are required to judge the number of this station. It may be necessary for the stations to be otherwise identified, perhaps by colours or by objects. The practical application of this activity for very handicapped children should be clear. They need to learn to move about their neighbourhoods independently if possible and with safety. An alert aural sense is needed to judge the proximity of traffic and other hazards.

The sequencing game suggested in chapter II is sometimes helpful in diagnostic and remedial work with cerebral palsied children, many of whom have specific learning disabilities. One very intelligent but severely handicapped boy in our school was very good at identifying individual sounds but very uncertain when asked to recall the order of as few as three sounds played consecutively. His other major area of difficulty was in spelling, and it seemed possible that these two problems were connected. Intensive remedial work involving much sequencing of a variety of everyday, instrumental, and vocal sounds was carried out, with a significant increase in his spelling ability. In his particular case, spelling was of great importance as he had no speech and often needed to communicate by means of an alphabet board.

With children who are at the phonic stage in reading it may be useful to sing vowel and diphthong sounds to them and to ask them to use these sounds in simple melodic phrases themselves. This is an additional and enjoyable way of focusing their attention on these sounds which need to be well internalised in order that they should be easily identified and recalled in the reading sessions. A simple game can be played to reinforce this work by drawing a number of objects and animals on the board, e.g. a car, a cow, a bow, a bed, a key, and a cat. The teacher sings the vowel involved in the name of each object or animal and the children have to indicate which picture the sound belongs to. The children may then be asked to sing vowels to be guessed, which helps to test their understanding and retentive powers. Singing the vowels might be regarded simply as an enjoyable alternative to saying them, but it is possible that some children will receive a clearer impression of the sound which is sung rather than spoken. In remedial teaching we need as many alternative

ways of presenting our material as possible; music can help us
to do this.

In conclusion, the following story should leave the reader in
no doubt about the value of music for our slow-learning and
handicapped children. Alec was a severely handicapped athetoid
boy who came to our school at the age of thirteen; he had
previously been placed in an ESN school near his home. His
speech was just intelligible and he had no useful movement of
limbs and, like many of these children, he had to be dressed,
fed, helped at the lavatory, and pushed around in his wheel-
chair. Shortly after his arrival we discovered that his means of
self-expression could be much extended by the use of a stick
which he held between his teeth—later on he had a moulded
dental piece to which the stick was joined. With this stick he
could use an electric typewriter, turn the pages of a book and
play a few table games. It was soon obvious that Alec was very
intelligent from the interest he displayed in everything around
and in the way he tackled the very limited range of activities
which were within his physical capabilities. He began to write
stories about space travel and spies and to read all he could lay
his 'hands' on. He was an intensive listener, especially to the
radio, and through this he discovered music of all kinds. For
some reason, any of the music of Wagner was especially meaningful to him and the stories associated with the works of this
composer sparked Alec's imagination. He desperately wanted to
play an instrument and to compose music himself. A mouth-
organ was mounted firmly on a stand and held to the table by
a suction pad so that he could be wheeled up to it and play it
by moving his head from side to side. The tubular bells were
more useful to him. These he played with his mouth stick, or
sometimes they were placed horizontally on a table so that he
could touch them with his nose to make them bounce on the
table. (These small tubular bells were individually suspended on
a pivot and could be moved like a see-saw when placed horizontally.)

Music became Alec's main centre of interest. He initiated the
school music club which met on certain evenings and listened to
classical records. He chose the music, wrote the programme notes,

and was chairman of the club. He had an excellent memory for
themes from the great works, and these stood him in good stead
when he took his Duke of Edinburgh award in music. For this
he needed to recognize or quote a dozen themes; his examiner
had to stop him after the fiftieth! After he left school, contact
was maintained with him and extracts from his letters tell the
rest of his story. He wrote on different occasions:
'there is a lot of work to be done before i take my GCE exams
next year but when i have some free time i turn to my favourite
hobby, music. if i am tense a slow piece of music will help me
to relax, i think this is because i am concentrating on the music
and i forget all about my problems. when i am feeling miserable,
a good rousing piece of music, like wagner, will make me feel
much brighter. i would say that music is a major part of my life,
and i would not go without music for anything in the world.

'i have had more tuition in music making and i learnt about the
chord structure of a tune. the three main chords were G C F.
with these chords came the joy of being able to play in a group.
i am now able to play more instruments than before. i took up
the xylophone which i play with my mouth stick and i use this
method also for the electric organ. with this success a group was
formed called 'why' and we have appeared before the school on
several occasions. the line up was organ, stylophone, chord organ,
maraca and drum.

'i have had great trouble in composing but now i have a new
system, e.g. DRMFSLTD = ABCDEFGA [*sic*]. hence i am able
to work out the notes and tell a person to write them down
instead of going through the embarrassment of having to sing.

'this year i have been to three operas—Wertha at Glyneborn and
two Gilbert and Sullivan, Iolanthe and Yeoman of the Guard and
i attended a Beethoven concert a few weeks ago and find that i
am much more relaxed at concerts than at operas.'

    Four years later, Alec wrote:
'Sorry I haven't written before but I got involved with my first
year exams (Open University degree) and you will be pleased
to know I passed and am now doing Sociology. I met X at the

summer school and we had some interesting talks and music sessions. I actually took part in some excerpts from 'Messiah' though my escort said I couldn't sing to save my life. The trouble was I couldn't read the music so I kept getting lost. I seem to be getting more progressive in my music and I am playing more instruments than I did at school. I am now living a more or less normal life and have the freedom to do what I like, when I like and how I like. I have a job in this hostel as Social Activities Officer and am trying to get the residents militant to get our rights in the hope that one day Society will accept us as people, not freaks.'

This boy at thirteen was by definition a slow learner. Clearly, there was a high level of intelligence in him, but it was imprisoned. How many handicapped children go through their schools without realising their potential abilities? The story of Alec highlights the important need to have teachers and resources for these children to at least give them the opportunity for developing their musical and other talents. In the long term it could well be that these become the real assets in their lives.

6   Music students' work with slow-learning children

We need to attract many more teachers to our special schools who have good practical skills which can be imparted to the children. The present shortage of music teachers in all schools should not be used as a reason to direct the flow of teacher recruits into ordinary schools as a priority. Slow-learning children can derive especial benefits from musical activity and they need the best teachers that can be found.

If we are to make educational provision according to the age, ability, and aptitude of all children, then we need to consider seriously that significant number of children whose learning difficulties are such that they need special educational treatment. The enormous advantages offered by special schools are possible because these schools are small, with seldom more than 180 pupils, and because the teachers are geared to the organization of individual and small group teaching. Unfortunately, this smallness sometimes limits the range of activities which are possible. In a staff of less than a dozen teachers it is difficult to find teaching skills to cover all the activities which are especially beneficial to our children. In one ESN school, the policy was to appoint teachers primarily on the basis of special skills such as music, art, drama, motor mechanics, heavy craftwork, home economics, outdoor pursuits, photography, and horticulture. The idea was that any of these teachers could learn, relatively quickly, how to teach reading and other 'basic' skills. The head and deputy head teachers had special training for work with slow-learning children and they were able to give much help and advice to newly appointed teachers on approaches to reading and number work. There was no evidence that the reading attainment of the children suffered in this school; there was, on the other hand, quite clear evidence of the children's high levels of achievement in the artistic, musical, and practical activities offered.

In our teacher-training courses we need to make arrangements for all our students to know about the needs of children in special schools, preferably through active participation and sufficiently long periods of observation. Many of our young students are very sensitive to the needs of handicapped and deprived children, and we should try to give them an insight into the ways in which provision and worthwhile contributions can be made.

At one college for potential music teachers, practical teaching sessions were an integral part of the students' programme. Each student spent several consecutive afternoon sessions with ESN children, usually in a team teaching situation, so that the maximum use was made of the time available.

For most of them, the main point of contact with the children was made through their 'main' musical instrument. As a starting point, and in order to stimulate the natural curiosity of the children, the students often placed their instrument, in its case, in front of the children and asked them to guess what was in the case. The younger ESN children usually knew the names of three instruments—the violin, trumpet, and guitar—and invariably hoped that one of these guesses would suffice. The instrument was then removed from its case and quickly assembled and a few sounds were made on it, sometimes with the children's help. Where possible, the children were allowed to hold the instrument. For most people musical instruments have an enormous appeal apart from the sounds they produce. These children in particular were enchanted by the shape, feel, and colour of the instruments; here was an excellent starting point.

The students often fell into the trap of becoming involved in abstract ideas about high and low, loud and soft sounds. 'High' was often confused with 'loud', by association with radio and television sets on which the volume may be turned 'up' or 'down'. Short complete pieces were usually enjoyed by the children, and music which evoked imagery was especially enjoyed. Some of the best sessions involved stories which were enriched by different instrumental sounds and short pieces. An account of one of these musical story sessions will illustrate how this was done.

The student, a violinist, told the children a story about a king who was always very sad and who would only become happy if he heard a magic violin play a particular tune. Several problems needed solving before this could happen—the instrument required an expert to tune it, another to tighten the bow, and another to apply the rosin. The king had to send for his expert courtiers (children selected from the class) who, with the student's help, solved each problem, but the violin remained silent until the last helper—an ordinary boy from the court kitchen—came and discovered that it was necessary to draw the bow across the strings! The eventual happy tune was 'Shepherd's Dance', from incidental music to *Henry VIII* by Edward German, which made the king happy ever after.

During subsequent visits, the students usually asked the children to talk about the previous week's session. There was a high level of retention, often strongly associated with the personality of the student and his instrument, and with the story he told. Our musical and other skills become a part of our whole personalities, and it is to these that the children can easily relate. The class teacher had a very important role to play in all these sessions by being quite involved and interested herself and by encouraging the children to continue talking about the sessions and to make associated pictures and writings after the students had left.

As an additional link between the sessions, a story and reading book was built up over the period of one or two school terms. 'Key' words in the children's own reading books and from the classroom wall charts were incorporated into this book, which also contained simple drawings of the instruments and incidents from the stories. A typical page would read:
'last week we had some visitors. they played the violin, the guitar and the oboe. they could not get in tune so they had to use a magic fork'.

The students found, sometimes to their dismay, that the children were surprisingly perceptive in their ability to judge a good performance. On one occasion, one of the children heard a student singing quite casually. This girl happened to be a student of singing and had a very beautiful voice. The child insisted that she sang a solo; he had immediately recognized her special skill.

These sessions made a great impression on the students. The

needs of the children and the problems encountered in teaching them were highlighted in the ESN class. It was vital for them to use words with simplicity and precision; any woolly approach was immediately seen to fail. One student asked the children 'how high' they thought his tuba could play. He received the disarming answer, 'ten feet!'. Other problems of presentation and class organisation were also clearly highlighted for the students. The need to play impromptu songs, to get away from the music copy, and to position themselves in order to retain the maximum contact with all the children was obvious. With small children, and those in wheelchairs, it was helpful to adopt a sitting or kneeling position in order to maintain facial and eye contact.

Partly as a result of their contact with special school work, a number of these students have become teachers of slow-learning children, or have maintained regular contact with handicapped children through their music. At the time or writing, several education authorities are trying to appoint peripatetic and advisory teachers who have responsibilities in a number of schools. This is an excellent way to solve the economic problem of supplying specialist teachers to small schools. The work is very challenging and demanding of energy and patience but it is hoped that many more music teachers will accept the challenge and consider working with slow-learning children who can derive such great benefits from musical activity.

To those who have read the preceding chapters, it should be clear that the teacher is the key figure in the overall pattern of musical provision for our slow-learning children. There is now a great variety of teacher-education and training courses from which recruits are drawn for the rather specialized work described in this book. Moreover, most establishments concerned with this education and training are looking for new ways to meet the staffing needs of schools.

For our particular work, we need teachers who are very good practical musicians and who have a sound knowledge of slow-learning children and how to teach them. Within the present and possible future patterns of education and training, how can we ensure that there will emerge teachers who are suited to undertake this work?

Musicians who are studying their art with a view to teaching need to develop good practical skills, if possible on more than one instrument. They should have a wide repertoire of pieces, many of which can be performed from memory. A good understanding of musical structures, styles, and idioms is required, so that music of the past and present can be performed and presented. An extensive knowledge of songs and a feeling for their appropriate use with all kinds of groups is necessary, together with an open and flexible mind which will see many possibilities for relating music to a wide variety of other activities.

Those who are to teach in special education need much practical experience of working and living with children who are variously handicapped. They need to become keen observers of children and careful students of the way children develop and behave in widely differing situations. This practical experience needs to be supported by much background reading on subjects such as child development, the causes, nature, and treatments of handicaps, and psychology.

It is unlikely that any training for work in special education can be completed in three years. Sufficient time is needed also for students to develop their own musical personalities. There seems to be a need for alternate periods of teaching experience and college study, both of which should firmly inter-relate. In the schools, student-teachers need advice and help from those who are more experienced and expert, together with opportunitie to observe good teaching in progress. The colleges might provide many more opportunities than at present for further study in depth of both music and special education.

By providing a long-term, flexible structure in further education and training, we should be able to attract both young and also more mature student-teachers into the profession. Sometimes the younger and less experienced can bring a freshness of approach to the schools; they often set out with no preconceptions which might lead to low expectations of the children's abilities.

1. *Gentle control*

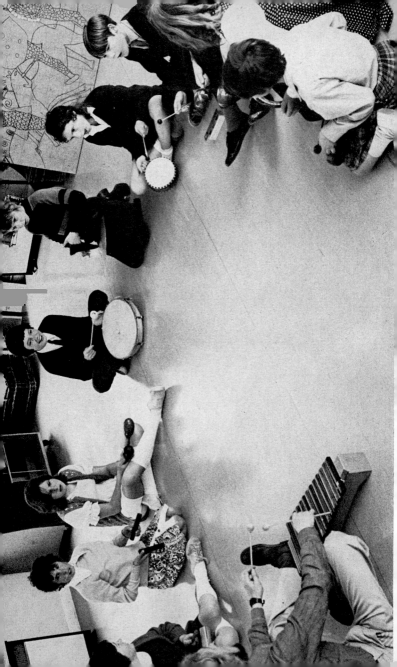

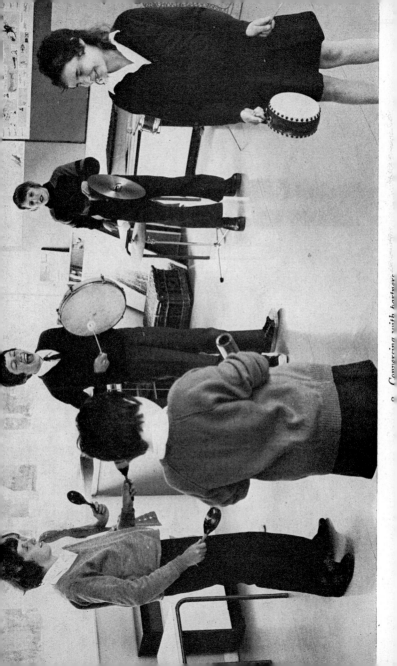

Conversing with partners

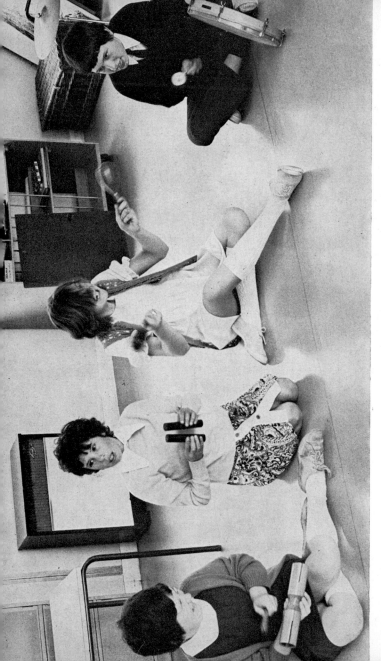

4 *Angry sounds*

5 *A good two-handed style*

6 *Body shapes*

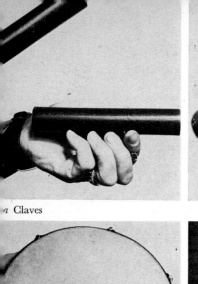

a Claves

b Maracas

c Tambour held in the hand

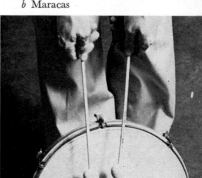

d Tambour secured by the foot

e Cymbal trill

f Xylophone—two-handed technique

Appendix I: The choice, use, and care of musical instruments

We should provide our children with the best instruments that can possibly be afforded. There is no justification whatsoever for giving less able children second-rate or discarded instruments. Generally speaking, with musical instruments, quality is directly related to cost, but for those who must consider the economics of instrument supply, the better instruments tend to be more durable. In one local special school, the cost of a good selection of instruments was worked out in relation to the number of children who used those instruments over a three-year period. This cost, in 1970, was about 2 pence per annum for each child.

If a limited budget is imposed, it seems wiser to invest in one or two good instruments than to buy a number of smaller and cheaper items. The educational advantages of doing so have been pointed out in the early chapters of this book. The durability of better instruments and the fact that they can be added to in following years support this suggestion in economic terms. It is, of course, possible to make instruments of very good quality in the school workshop. For those who are interested in combining excellent craftsmanship with music, Ronald Roberts' book *Musical instruments made to be played* (Dryad Press) is invaluable.

Cymbals should be large—at least 10" in diameter—and should be correctly equipped with a leather strap which is properly tied. They should not be played with metallic strikers—although wire brushes are allowed—and never left to lie around flat on the floor. A good many cymbals have been completely ruined by an accidental heavy boot! If possible, two or three different-sized cymbals should be available for making a variety of effects; if a matched pair can also be provided this will enable selected players to practise basic orchestral techniques. A simple and secure cymbal stand is necessary, so that the players can use two beaters or brushes or 'double' on other instruments.

Triangles should be tried out, if possible, before they are chosen. Some of the larger versions sold at present are too heavy for many of our children to hold. Bigger is not better where these particular instruments are concerned. Always ensure that correctly designed holders are to hand. These holders should have fairly stiff gut loops which prevent the triangle from swinging round when played. Although a six-inch nail will do the job of a striker, a proper chromium-plated beater with a rubber end is much better! It has the advantage of ensuring a secure grip, and also of allowing the player to use the rubber end to strike the instrument for soft sounds and to bring out the lower harmonics. Two triangles are sufficient for most percussion ensembles.

Chime bars, tubular bells, glockenspiels, and metallophones all fulfil similar tonal requirements. The obvious advantage of chime bars is that they can be arranged in a great variety of ways; each child can be given exactly as many bars as he can cope with. With all the tuned percussion instruments, attention has to be given to the actual tuning; one cannot assume that the different models available will be properly in tune. Check the individual bars of one instrument with another; if a distinct vibration, or tuner's beat, is discerned then another choice should be made. It may be necessary to enlist the help of a fellow musician who has a keen ear to confirm the intonation of the instruments. A variety of pairs of beaters is needed. By trial and error the teacher will discover the most suitable pairs for each instrument. Many music teachers like to keep a chosen pair of beaters with each individual glockenspiel. A good system needs to be devised for keeping the extra bars of glockenspiels together; much time can be wasted in hunting for appropriate bars, and it goes without saying that one lost bar may mean that the instrument is useless. Do not allow metal strikers to be used on chime bars and bells. Not only does this spoil the appearance of the instruments but it also affects the tuning.

Much of what has been said about the metallic instruments with bars is also applicable to the xylophones (Greek: xylon = wood). Examine the method by which the bars are attached and, all other things being equal, choose the model which has its bars most securely attached. There is a tendency for the bars to jump off unless they are struck exactly in the middle.

The classroom collection should include as many different-sized drums as possible. A small snare drum and stand are very desirable, and the drum should have a reliable mechanism for quick application and release of the snares. Drums which have screw devices to enable them to be tuned should have the screw heads, wing nuts, or 'taps' easily accessible. Some of these have their tuning screws inside the drum, which does not allow for quick and easy tuning. Ensure that the drum heads are reduced in tension when they are stored, and remember that heat causes most heads to tighten significantly. This fact should be remembered when the instruments are being used in different rooms for performances. In cold, damp weather it may be necessary to warm the heads gently in order to restore the tension which is needed to produce sounds at the required (approximate) pitch. When storing drums, beware of hard and sharp-edged objects which may puncture the skins.

Several pairs of matching maracas are desirable. If the sounds made by individual maracas in any pair are slightly different, consider this an advantage as it helps players to practise interesting patterns with alternate left and right hand actions. Warn the children against dropping their instruments on a hard floor. Maracas are easily cracked and are difficult to secure in a cramp for glueing.

The Japanese castanets which are widely available are the best models for school use. These are secured and tensioned by a piece of rubber which makes them spring apart immediately after they are tapped together. For physically handicapped children, they can be mounted on a board or on a foam pad, placed upon a table, and tapped with only a very small movement.

A variety of sleigh bells is useful. Try to obtain some which are attached to straps, stout wooden hoops, straight sticks, etc. This makes for a variety of ways of holding them or attaching them to limbs which may have spastic movements.

Guiros—hollow bamboo sticks with notches filed along the length—are excellent for both rhythmic work and sound effects. They are played with a hard stick; a metal triangle striker is permissible, but ensure that the children do not use it for other instruments.

Wood-blocks are produced in various designs. The two-tone

Chinese blocks presently available are cheap and make excellent sounds. They are usually supplied with a wooden striker of correct size and weight but a wooden ball xylophone beater may be used as an alternative.

Claves are simply pairs of hard wooden dowel about 1" in diameter and 9" long. They should normally make sounds of slightly different pitch, and are played by placing one on the fingertips of an upturned hand which is relaxed and cupped in such a way that it acts as a simple resonator. See illustration 8a. The second clave is used as a striker.

Tambourines should not be too large for easy manipulation by the young children. Check that they are sturdily constructed, particularly in the way the head is attached to the hoop. The jingles are usually held in position by a central pin, which can be dangerous if loose.

Crotals, or Indian finger cymbals should only be played by tapping the rims together. They tend to make very unpleasant sounds if 'clapped' or allowed to clatter on a hard table top.

Recorders are now produced in hard plastic which is unbreakable. The Japanese models are especially well tuned and easy to play. They should not be left lying around in odd corners; hygiene is essential. Devise simple bags for them if the original containers are discarded. The children need to be shown how to clean them with a recorder brush after use. Like all wind instruments, they should not be passed around for everyone to play.

It is not possible, in the space available, to describe all the techniques needed for the playing of the percussion instruments, but it is hoped that the following hints will be generally helpful.

A good style in beater technique is essential; if early attention is paid to the way beaters are gripped and moved, this will assist in the playing of many percussion instruments. Two-handed playing is to be encouraged wherever possible. Select a pair of matching beaters and hold them confidently between the thumb and first finger of each hand, so that the shaft of the beater lies naturally in the 'fold' of the finger. By experimentation the most convenient point of balance along the beater shaft will be found, but this is likely to be at a point about $\frac{2}{3}$ the way along the shaft (away from the head). The beater should be held in such a way that it can be quickly moved up and down with a neat wrist movement. Practise alternate left and right beats on a drum, beginning slowly and gradually increasing the speed of the beats. Still with the two beaters held in the same way, practise simple scale passages on the xylophone, using left and right hands alternately to ascend and descend the scale. See illustration 8f. Clearly, for any individual melodic phrase, a little thought needs to be given to the way in which left/right patterns are achieved. The teacher will be surprised at the rapid increase in confidence once this style is established. This left/right 'matched grip' is used in the playing of xylophones, glockenspiels, chime bars, snare drums, timpani, and suspended cymbal. It is also the basis of the playing of rhythmic patterns on the maracas, which are gripped in exactly the same way, i.e. between the thumb and first finger, but in this case quite near the bulb of the instrument. The shaft should fall naturally into the palm of the hand. See illustration 8b. Always try to make the beater *bounce* off the instrument. Sometimes young children do not understand that when vibrations have been set up in the bars of the instrument, the beater must be immediately taken off to allow them to continue.

Drums of all kinds need to be thoughtfully placed for various ways of playing and to gain special effects. The tambour, which is a single-headed drum, is usually held away from the body and struck at a point which is about halfway between the very centre and the perimeter of the head. See illustration 8c. In this way, a confident, bouncing blow will produce a sound of fairly definite pitch as long as the head is suitably tensioned. The children are usually fascinated by the way the tambour 'sings' back its own note when the voice is pitched to it and directed onto the skin. This is the standard method of checking the tuning of orchestral tympani; if the children ever have the opportunity to observe a professional tympanist they can be advised to watch this fascinating procedure. If the tambour skin is damped by holding it near the body, or by placing a clean handkerchief at the back and touching the skin, an interesting damped effect can be obtained using either the beater or the fingertips. A novel but useful way to enable the tambour to be played with two beaters

is to position it vertically on the floor, securing it carefully with
the toe of one foot. See illustration 8d.

Tambourines and maracas can be played in a number of ways
which involve shaking the instruments or tapping them with a
free hand. They may also be lightly tapped on the knee or with
the fingertips to achieve a precise, quiet effect.

The triangle is mostly struck on the outside, near the apex.
A 'trill' is achieved by placing the striker inside the triangle, in
one angled corner and by rapidly moving the striker from side
to side. For a trill on the suspended cymbal, a rapid left/right
action may be employed. Otherwise, two beaters held forklike
above and below the cymbal, near the rim, may be quickly
activated by a wrist movement to produce the rapid alternation
of blows necessary to produce the trill. See illustration 8e.

If a drum roll is required, an approximation can be gained
by a 'scrubbing' action of left and right sticks. A few of our
children will wish to learn to play the snare drum in the military
style; sometimes they, or their brothers join Boys' Brigade
bands and very much enjoy the discipline of this kind of
drumming. By all means try to get special tuition for them, but
the teacher will generally prefer to concentrate on the matched
grip technique already described. This technique is favoured by
many present day leading percussionists. Teachers who are
interested in furthering their percussion techniques are advised
to refer to *Orchestral percussion technique* by James Blades
(O.U.P.) who is well known for his expertise on this subject and
for his excellent talks and demonstrations to handicapped childre

Teachers should give some thought to the way musical instruments are stored when not in use. More damage occurs to instruments in store than in use, and the percussion instruments
quickly become unsightly if they are carelessly left around to
become scratched, chipped, and dusty. Store cupboards should
be easily accessibie so that the larger instruments can be quickly
removed for use with waiting classes. Many schools have an
instrument trolley which holds almost all the instruments which
are regularly needed. If music lessons happen in several rooms,
this is an excellent way to store the instruments quickly and to
save time in transportation. It is a good idea to train the children

to carry the instruments carefully and to replace them in an orderly way after use.

The care displayed in choosing, storing, and playing musical instruments of all kinds is often an indication of the importance teachers and their children give to the music which is produced. Part of our job is to impart a love for the instruments of music as well as for the beautiful sounds they can produce.

Appendix II: List of songs, music books, and records

The following songs have all been successfully performed by ESN children. The songs often appear in more than one book; care has been taken to involve the use of the minimum number of books and to select versions which are well presented. It may be necessary to transpose many of the songs into keys which suit the children's vocal range and which are convenient for various instrumental accompaniments.

The list is divided into two sections according to broad age ranges, but this should not prevent teachers from trying out some of the 'younger' songs with older children. We cannot always be sure how the meaning and feeling of a song will affect individuals and particular groups; sometimes we find that the older children enjoy songs which they sang as infants, perhaps for nostalgic reasons, and many of the older girls might be encouraged to revise nursery songs as part of their preparatory courses in home economics and child care.

Songs for younger children

The Oxford Nursery Song Book P. Buck O.U.P.
This book contains all the well-known nursery rhymes

American Folk-Songs for Children R. Seeger Doubleday
Mr Frog's wedding	The mocking bird song
Jimmy crack corn	Who built the ark?
Mary wore her red dress	Johnnie get your hair cut
Who's that tapping at the window?	There was a man and he was mad
The train is a-coming	

Music Time M. Wilson O.U.P.
Jackie the sailor	The donkey and the cuckoo
Susie, little Susie	

The Oxford School Music Books R. Fiske and J. Dobbs O.U.P.
Junior Book 1
There's a young lad	Bobby Shaftoe
Sing said the mother	Boney was a warrior
The drummer and the cook	Down in Demerara
Go and tell Aunt Nancy	

Junior book 2

The keeper	Nelly Bly
O, soldier, soldier	Sourwood Mountain
Oh, my little Augustin	

Junior book 3

Donkey riding

Sixty Songs for Little Children   H. Wiseman and J. Wishart   O.U.P.
My three hens

Sing Together   W. Appleby and F. Fowler   O.U.P.

The gay musician	Jim along Josie
Ten in the bed	The barnyard song
This old man	Skip to my Lou
The noble Duke of York	The cuckoo
Tree in the wood	Michael Finnegan
Turn the glasses over	Leave her Johnny

Folk-Songs for Fun   O. Brand   Essex Music

The hole in the bucket	Aiken drum
Old MacDonald	

Sing a Merry Song   B. Swift and W. Clauson   O.U.P.
Let's all sing together

Sing a New Song   Orff-Schulwerk   Schott

Looby Loo	Row, row, row your boat (a round)

Children's Play Songs   P. Nordoff and C. Robbins   Theodore Presser Co.,
Pennsylvania

All the songs in this book are suitable

Songs for older children

Sing Together   W. Appleby and F. Fowler   O.U.P.

Li'l Liza Jane	What shall we do with the drunken sailor?
A-roving	Fire down below
John Brown's body	Waltzing Matilda
The mermaid	Green grow the rushes-o
I'se the b'y that builds the boat	

Something to Sing   G. Brace   C.U.P.
Book 1

Jesse James	Casey Jones
Jamaica farewell	The sloop John B
This old hammer	

Book 2
Yellow rose of Texas

A Pentatonic Song Book B. Brocklehurst   Schott
Old Dan Tucker   Little David
Swing low sweet chariot   Land of the silver birch
One more river   The Derby ram

Faith, Folk and Clarity   edited by P. Smith   Galliard
The Lord's prayer   Kumbayah
Lord of the dance   Go, tell it on the mountain
Thank you   Amen

124 Folk-Songs   Robbins Music Corporation
Down in the valley   Joshua fought the battle of Jericho
Oleanna   Red river valley
Tom Dooley   This little light of mine
Study war no more   Pick a bale o' cotton

104 Folk-Songs   Robbins Music Corporation
Oh, sinner man   Michael, row the boat ashore
We shall overcome   Streets of Laredo

Folk-Songs for Fun   O. Brand   Essex Music
When the saints go marching in   Goodnight ladies
When I first came to this land   Ten green bottles
Alouette   Blow the man down
Pat works on the railway

Songs of the New World   D. MacMahon   Holmes McDougall
Home on the range   Johnny has gone for a soldier

Twelve Folk-Songs from Jamaica   edited by T. Murray   O.U.P.
Wata come to me eye   Banana loader's song
Linstead market

The American Folk-Song Book   Penguin books
The hammer song   It takes a worried man to sing a
                                   worried song

The Oxford School Music Books   R. Fiske and J. Dobbs   O.U.P.
Junior book 3

The lone star trail

American Folk-Songs for Children   R. Seeger   Doubleday
Mary had a baby

Cantatas

Jonah Man Jazz   M. Hurd   Novello

Joseph and the Amazing Technicolor Dreamcoat   T. Rice and A. Lloyd-
                                    Webber   Novello

Song of Caedmon and *The Shepherd's Tale*   I. Kendell   Chester

Musical Plays

The midnight thief   R. R. Bennett   Belwyn Mills Music

The snow wolf   M. Williamson   Josef Weinberger

The following books are recommended for further sources of songs, ideas for accompaniments, and hints on teaching:

Ears and Eyes Books I and II   J. Dobbs, R. Fiske, and M. Lane   O.U.P.
An excellent collection of songs with pictures and poems to stimulate interest in the topics associated with the songs.

Sociable Songs Books I and II   edited by A. Mendoza   O.U.P.
Songs with simple piano accompaniments, guitar chords, and symbols; hints on teaching.

People who Help us   E. Hughes   Novello
Songs about the bus driver, policeman, etc; easy piano accompaniments.

Things that Help us   E. Hughes   Novello
Songs about toys, books, cars, etc.

Our friends the animals   E. Hughes   Novello
Animal songs; easy accompaniments.

Music Makers Stages 1, 2 and 3   M. Berry   Longman
Mainly about the use of musical notation, in large, clear print.

Rhymes with Chimes   O. Rees and A. Mendoza   O.U.P.
Simple songs with easy parts for chime bars and other percussion.

Children Make Music   R. Addison   Holmes McDougall
A handbook of practical suggestions for a variety of music activities.

Ring-a-Ding: Songs with tuned percussion   Y. Adair   Novello
Very simple two-note accompaniments using chimes.

Singing Games for Recreation Books I—IV   J. E. Tobitt   A & C Black
Well-known and unusual singing games, melody only, with instructions for actions.

Children's Traditional Singing Games   Books 1—5   Gomme and Sharp
Novello

The Clarendon Book of Singing Games   Books 1 & 2   H. Wiseman and
S. Northcote   O.U.P.

Children's Games in Street and Playground   P. and I. Opie   O.U.P.

The Oxford School Music Books   Infant book   J. Dobbs and W. Firth
O.U.P.

The Oxford School Music Books   Teacher's manual   R. Fiske and
J. Dobbs   O.U.P.
A variety of suggestions to help the music teacher, including basic piano
and recorder tuition.

An Introduction to Group Music Making   G. Winters   Chappell
A handbook of advice and suggestions about the use of school instruments.

Three Chords and Beyond   R. Noble   Novello
A useful book for the teacher's own use; contains melodies with two-
and three-chord accompaniments for guitar or piano.

Records

Unfortunately the availability of any record cannot be guaranteed.
The following discs have proved very useful with slow learning
children:

Growing up with Wally Whyton   Pye GGL 0285

Gospel Songs and Spirituals for Little Children—from the Salvation Army,
101 Queen Victoria Street, London EC4

Songs for Singing Children by John Langstaff   EMI XLP 50008

Singing Games and Party Songs for Children by John Langstaff   EMI
7EJ266

Bang on a Drum—a BBC Playschool record   BBC Roundabout No 17

Children's Singing Games collected by Mary Wilson and Jennifer Gallagher
Topic records—IMP(act) A101

Songs for Children by Mary Rowland, Pat Shaw, James Blades, and
Joan Rimmer   Argo DA 32

Joseph and the Amazing Technicolor Dreamcoat   Rice and Webber
Decca SKL 4973

Dances for Swinging Children   Dennis Darke   ED 111 from English Folk Dance and Song Society, Cecil Sharp House, 2 Regents Park Road, London NW1

English Folk Dancing in the Primary School   EFDSS (see above)   BR 3

Listen, Move and Dance   Nos 1 and 2   HMV 7EG8727 —28

Appendix III: Books related to music for slow-learning children

Alvin, J. *Music therapy* Hutchinson, 1974

Alvin, J. *Music for the handicapped child* O.U.P., 1965

Alvin, J. *Music therapy for severely sub-normal boys* British Society for Music Therapy, 1970

Bailey, P. *They can make music* O.U.P., 1970

Blocksidge, K. M. *Making musical instruments* The Nursery Schools Association (89 Stamford St., London SE1)

Brocklehurst, J. B. *Music in schools* (Chapter VIII) Routledge and Kegan Paul, 1962

Bruce, V. *Dance and drama in education* Pergamon, 1965

Carlson, B. W. and Gingland, D. R. *Play activities for the retarded child* Bailliere, Tindall and Cassell, 1962

Dobbs, J. P. B. *The slow learner and music* O.U.P., revised 1974

Gaston, E. Thayer *Music in therapy* Collier-Macmillan, 1968

Gingland, D. R. and Stiles, W. *Music activities for retarded children* Bailliere, Tindall and Cassell, 1965

Gray, V. and Percival, R. *Music, movement, and mime for children* O.U.P., 1962

McLeish, J. and Higgs, J. *An inquiry into the musical capacities of ESN children* Cambridge Institute of Education, 1967

Nordoff, P. and Robbins, C. *Therapy in music for handicapped children* Gollancz, 1971

Priestley, M. *Music therapy in action* Constable, 1974

Roberts, R. *Musical instruments Made to be Played* Dryad Press, 1968

Robins, F. and J. *Educational rhythmics for mentally handicapped children* Ra-Verlag, Rapperswill, Switzerland, 1967

Shuter, R. *The psychology of musical ability* Methuen, 1968

Ward, D. *Singing in special schools* RPS Ltd., Victoria Hall, East Greenwich, London SE 10

Ward, D. *Sound approaches for slow learners* as above

Department of Education and Science *Music in Schools* (Chapter VI) Pamphlet no. 27, 1969

Disabled Living Foundation *Music and the physically handicapped* (i) Report of investigations. (ii) Conference report 1970

London University Institute of Education *Handbook for Music Teachers* (Chapter 2 deals with special education) General editor B. Rainbow Novello, 1968

Appendix IV: General information

Information about full-time and part-time courses which deal with music in special education can be obtained from The Music Department, Dartington College of Arts, Totnes, Devon.

The Guildhall School of Music and Drama, London, offers a one-year course in music therapy. Applicants for this course need to have good keyboard facility and instrumental ability of degree or diploma standard. Further information about this course may be obtained from The Secretary, British Society for Music Therapy, 48 Lanchester Road, London N6 or The Guildhall School of Music, John Carpenter Street, London EC4.

Local education authorities often provide courses for music teachers in their schools. These may be helpful to teachers who deal with slow-learning children. Enquiries are normally made to the music adviser at the local authority education office.

The Department of Education and Science is responsible for a number of long and short courses and publishes an annual programme of these courses. The programme and additional information about relevant publications can be obtained from the Department's headquarters, Teachers' Branch IIL, Elizabeth House, 39 York Road, London SE1.

The British Broadcasting Corporation's publishing section offers a wide range of books and records on many subjects, and their programmes for schools and students are excellent. The BBC's address for publications is 35, Marylebone High Street, London W1.

order end